THE IMITATION OF CHRIST

Christian Classics in the Paraclete Living Library Series

Fénelon: Meditations on the Heart of God
François Fénelon
Eighty-five encouraging reflections on how to seek God in everyday life.

Fénelon: Talking with God
François Fénelon
Guidance from a great spiritual director on true prayer of the heart and union with God.

So Amazing, So Divine: A Guide to Living Prayer
Isaac Watts
The great 18th-century hymn writer speaks a clear and needed word to all who seek to learn to pray.

Life Secrets
Henry Foster
Mature insights of a 19th-century Christian physician who spent his life serving Christ and others.

Confessions of St. Augustine
One of Christendom's greatest classics, rendered into clear modern English.

The Pilgrim's Progress
John Bunyan
A mildly modernized version with 19th-century illustrations.

The Practice of the Presence of God
Brother Lawrence
An easy to read translation by Robert Edmonson.

The Joy of Full Surrender
Jean Pierre de Caussade
A modern English version of *L'Abandon à la Providence Divine.*

The Royal Way of the Cross
François Fénelon
Fifty-two letters of spiritual counsel by Fénelon.

THE IMITATION OF CHRIST

THOMAS À KEMPIS

REVISED TRANSLATION

EDITED BY HAL M. HELMS

PARACLETE PRESS
BREWSTER, MASSACHUSETTS

20 19 18 17 16

Library of Congress #: 82-61908
ISBN 10: 0-941478-07-6
ISBN 13: 978-0-941478-07-6

Published by Paraclete Press
Brewster, Massachusetts
www.paracletepress.com

Printed in the United States of America.

Table of Contents

Book I

Admonitions Useful for a Spiritual Life

Book II

Admonitions Concerning the Inner Life

Book III

On Internal Consolation

Book IV

Concerning the Sacrament

INTRODUCTION

The Imitation of Christ has enjoyed an unparalleled place in the world of books for more than five hundred years, second only to the Bible itself. It has been termed "a chief companion piece to the Bible." Estimates of the number of published editions run between three and five thousand, and it is said to have been translated into almost every language in the world.

The message of this humble volume has attracted readers and admirers as diverse as Ignatius of Loyola, founder of the Jesuit Order, and John Wesley, father of Methodism. The great Englishman of letters, Dr. Johnson, was an admirer of it, as was Sir Thomas More and General Gordon of the Sudan. Readers of Agatha Christie may recall that Miss Marple's bedtime reading was often from the *Imitation,* and George Eliot, who referred to it as "a small, oldfashioned book," featured its healing influence in one of her novels, *The Mill on the Floss.*

Although in recent years it has been attacked by some as being too introspective, it nevertheless continues on as a bestseller in our day. A glance at the present list of *Books in Print* shows more than a dozen editions currently available to American readers.

Like other books of timeless value, its beginnings are obscure, and it has been attributed to several different authors in the course of its long history. The name we most commonly associate with it, and the man to whom we owe its present structure, is a fifteenth-century monk, Thomas Hammerken, better known as Thomas à Kempis. Its particular spirituality, however, derives from the life and work of two other men, Gerard Groote (1340-1384) and Florentius Radewyn (1350-1400), founders of the Brethren of the Common Life.

Brethren of the Common Life

Gerard Groote was born at Deventer, Holland, of wealthy parents, and attended the University of Paris where he made a brilliant record, becoming a canonist, or expert in Church law. He taught for some time at Cologne, Germany, living in great luxury and self-indulgence until, in 1374, he experienced a profound spiritual awakening and "began to live a devout and simple life." He spent some three years in a monastery, and was ordained to preach throughout the Netherlands as a deacon, and licensed by the Bishop of Utrecht. His message was a call to repentance and a renewal of devotion to Jesus. The common people heard him gladly, overfilling churches, and necessitating open air meetings to hear his heart-stirring messages. But his forthright attack on the corrupt and indulgent lifestyle of the clergy provoked enmity in high places, and at the instigation of jealous men in the Church, he was silenced twice by the Bishop of Utrecht.

Some of his followers, however, went with him back to his home town of Deventer, and formed a little association to live out what they had heard. They called themselves The Brethren of the Common Life. A few were clergy, but most were lay people, all of whom were expected to earn their own way, for Gerard opposed any idea of depending on the alms of others for their subsistence. Their main calling was to copy the Holy Scriptures and other spiritual books, and to spread the message of repentance and devotion to Christ which Gerard had sounded. In those days, the only way to reproduce a book was to copy it by hand, and the calling of the copyist was a noble one, for it was his privilege to make the words and truths of the Holy Scriptures and of the saints available to thousands.

While the clergy busied themselves teaching school (they

became famous for their free schools throughout the land), preaching, and conducting services especially among the poor, the lay brothers tilled the soil, made shoes, cloth, and baskets, and did a variety of other things useful to their life. Although they took no vows, they were dedicated to a life of poverty, chastity, and obedience. In addition to the association of men at Deventer, there were groups of women who began to follow the same course.

Florentius Radewyn had been impressed with Gerard's message, and was led to examine his own life. As a result, he resigned his position as canon of the cathedral at Utrecht, and followed Gerard to Deventer. There he became Gerard's colleague, and eventually his successor as leader of the infant community. At the beginning, the brethren did not live together under one roof, but Florentius felt more and more that this should be the next step, pooling their earnings and living a common life.

"Live together?" responded Gerard. "The Mendicants would never allow it!" (The Mendicants had been responsible for the revoking of his license to preach, and were a powerful force in the Church.)

"But what is to prevent our trying?" Florentius persisted. "Perhaps God will give us success."

And so it came about. It was to this little brotherhood that Thomas à Kempis was sent when he was twelve years old. Gerard had died and Florentius was then director of the Community. Thomas describes the Brethren of the Common Life as follows:

"[They were] humble men of God without a spark of worldliness about them. Abiding quietly at home, they busied themselves in copying books, especially the sacred Scriptures; engaging in devout meditations, they obtained comfort and refreshment in the midst of their labors by having recourse to ejaculatory prayers or short aspirations of the soul. Early in the morning they went to church and said the office of matins. Holding obedience to be the highest rule of life, they endeavored with all their might to conquer self, to subdue their evil passions, and to break the motions of their own will. Great grace and true devotion were among them, and they edified many, both by their word and example; and by patiently bearing the derision of those who were in bondage to the world, they won over many to a contempt of worldly things. . . . " (Thomas à Kempis, *Life of Florentius,* as quoted by Kettlewell, pp. 116,117)

It was in the Brotherhouse, according to his own words, that Thomas "learned to write," an art which prepared him to become a copyist, in which he spent most of his life.

Within a short time there were several houses of Brothers and Sisters of the Common Life. The misguided zeal of two or three brothers convinced Gerard and Florentius that some more definite institution was needed to supply ongoing direction and stability to the work. A path of wisdom needed to be found which would not result in spiritual anarchy, schism or heresy. Their desire was to promote repentance and change *within* the Church, not apart from it.

Gerard wavered between seeking connection with the Carthusians or the Cistercians, two Orders that demanded a high degree of commitment from their members. Seeking further counsel, Gerard went to a monastery near Brussels, where one of the most outstanding spiritual leaders of the time was prior, Jan van Ruysbroek. Ruysbroek advised that a way be found which would be moderate, and not too severe for Gerard's followers, and apparently suggested the Augustinian Canons Regular as a good choice. The Augustinian spirituality seemed particularly well suited to Gerard's vision of what he hoped his movement would be, and the decision was made to found a house or monastery among his disciples.

The rule of St. Augustine does indeed seek to provide that "middle way" between too much laxity and too much severity (see Appendix).

It can be readily seen how much of the Augustinian spirituality pervades *The Imitation of Christ.*

Before the plan could be carried through, Gerard Groote contracted the plague and died, leaving Florentius to carry out the plans they had made. Six of the *devoti* ("devoted ones") spent some time at an Augustinian monastery, took their vows, and formed the first house at Windesheim, near Zwolle, Holland. Florentius remained behind with the Brethren at Deventer. From this time on, the Canons Regular formed a core of the fellowship, with groups of lay Brethren at the periphery living a common life, coming and going as their work required. It was a very successful arrangement, and it was through these fellowships that *The Imitation of Christ* spread so quickly after its initial appearance.

As it happened, the Brethren of the Common Life did not survive long after Thomas's own generation. The invention of the printing press in the middle of the fifteenth century abruptly made copying, their main vocation, obsolete, and "their wholesome and simple piety was swept into the enthusiasms of the Reformation to be either fulfilled or frustrated in the happenings of the sixteenth century." (Willard Sperry, *Strangers and Pilgrims,* p. 76)

Thomas à Kempis

Thomas Hammerken was born in 1380 in Kempin, a small, walled town near Cologne, Germany. His brother, John, fifteen years his senior, went early into the religious life. When Thomas was twelve, he went at his brother's advice to Deventer, where Florentius received him, and provided schooling, housing, books, and board for the next seven years. He attended the village school, run by the brothers, sang in the choir, and "learned to write," joining the noble copyists at their work.

After his training at Deventer, Thomas went in 1399, with Florentius's blessing, to Mount St. Agnes, the first daughterhouse of Windesheim, where his brother John had been cofounder, and was now prior. Florentius sent a request that the rule against having two brothers in the same monastery be set aside in their case, and it was done. Here Thomas spent the rest of his long life. He waited six years before becoming a novice, and on June 10, 1406, he made his solemn profession as an Augustinian Canon Regular. Seven more years would pass before he was ordained, at the age of thirty-three.

Once we hear of his traveling to Windesheim on business. In 1429 he accompanied the rest of the brethren in their migration to Ludenkerk, to avoid the papal interdict that Windesheim suffered as a result of a disputed canonical election. During this absence, Thomas was called away from Ludenkerk to the Convent of Bethany, to care for his dying brother, John. Altogether he was away from Mount St. Agnes for about three years out of seventy-two. "Twice he was sub-prior, once he was procurator [or bursar] of the community, but the business of these offices fretted him, and he appears to have been glad to fall back into the quiet round of copying good books, writing his little treatises, teaching his novices, and meditating in his beloved cell." (Bigg, pp. 21, 22)

It had been the practice of Gerard Groote and Florentius to encourage the brothers to keep a book of extracts from their readings–pithy and meaningful sayings and thoughts gleaned mainly from their reading. Gerard set the example himself, and has, indeed, been credited by some as being the real author of this book. Without doubt, his practice of encouraging the keeping of *raparia*, as these books were called, lies behind the book. Since the *raparia* were kept for the good of all, Thomas would have had access not only to his own book, but to those of others, greatly expanding the numbers of authors who would become known to him. It is not surprising, therefore, that we find allusions or quotations from St. Augustine, St. Bernard of Clairvaux, St. Francis of Assisi, St. Thomas Aquinas, St. Bonaventura, St. Gregory the Great, and even from such classical authors as Aristotle, Ovid, and Seneca. There are also echoes of medieval Latin hymns, and "you can scarcely read a sentence," said one observer, "that does not recall some passage, now in the Old, now in the New Testament."

"If it be mainly quotation," says Dean Sperry, "it is 'inspired quotation.' It is a single, closely wrought work, wanting perhaps in novelty but marked by profound originality." (Sperry, p. 65)

Apart from his historical sources, even remembrances which the author quotes unconsciously, there is the stamp of immediate inspiration and the spark of fire of a soul that is turned to God and is listening to what the Spirit is saying. When he says, "I will hear what the Lord God will speak in me" (Book III, Chapter 1), we can believe that he means exactly that, and that he is listening in spirit to the inner voice of the Consoler and Strengthener of Christians, the Holy Spirit.

From many references in the *Imitation*, it is obvious that Thomas practiced what he preached. When he expresses concern about those who compete with one another as to whose saint is the greatest, he is undoubtedly letting us glimpse some of the malaise of his time—the competition for honor and prestige among monasteries and convents. But he prefers to leave all honors and preferments to God.

When he talks about those who run about from shrine to

shrine, he reflects the fascination for pilgrimage characteristic of his century. But he confesses that he has seldom "gone abroad," meaning outside the monastery, without returning home less a man than he was. And he observes that he sees little fruit or amendment in the lives of those who busy themselves rushing about to see and hear new things.

When he talks about the need for repentance before God, we can hear the sorrow and grief of his own heart, as he reviews his own sin and unworthiness before the Holy of Holies.

So the book transcends its time, and geographical origins, even the author's individuality, and becomes a document for all times, speaking to the perennial human condition and dealing with the issues of our human need and the transforming power of Jesus Christ. Where others seek a different world, Thomas seeks a different self. His calling is to live each day in simple obedience to the Lord, and to pursue his daily tasks in the knowledge that only a changed heart can result in any lasting change for good. Some critics have criticized him as being essentially self-centered. They should look again at the profound and lasting influence this book has had over the past five hundred years. His words and thoughts have served as a stabilizing ballast for many others who have felt called to a more "active" life in the world and have plunged into the fray, to fight or work for change and progress in other ways.

The Imitation of Christ is a perpetual reminder that action—without humility and without a realistic sense of our human condition—will always in the long run be a "tale full of sound and fury, signifying nothing." On the other hand, this book should be an encouragement to those who seem destined to live out their lives in hidden, unnoticed places, with no great achievements to mark up to their credit, and no lasting fame to attach to their names.

"He shows us," says Kettlewell, "how the life of a Christian in ordinary circumstances may be made lovely by the cultivation of the spiritual life. . . ." That should be justification enough for any book!

—Hal M. Helms

The Translation

The present version is a revised translation, which has made use of all available English versions for comparison with the Latin text of Hirsche, based on the 1441 manuscript in Thomas à Kempis's own hand.

The First Book

Admonitions Useful for a Spiritual Life

Chapter 1

On the Imitation, or Following of Christ, and Contempt of All the Vanities of the World

He who follows Me," says the Lord, "will not walk in darkness but will have the light of life."[1] These are the words of Christ, by which we are taught to follow His life and way of life if we would be truly enlightened and delivered from all blindness of heart. Let it therefore be our chief endeavor to meditate upon the life of Jesus Christ.

2. The teaching of Jesus Christ excels all the teachings of the saints; and he who has the Spirit, will find therein the hidden manna.[2]

But it happens that many, although they often hear the Gospel of Christ, are yet but little moved by it, because they do not have the Spirit of Christ.

Whoever, then, would fully and wholeheartedly understand the words of Christ, must endeavor to conform his life entirely to the life of Christ.

3. What will you gain if you dispute learnedly on the doctrine of the Trinity, if you lack humility, and are thereby displeasing to the Trinity?

Surely great words do not make a man holy and righteous; but a virtuous life makes him dear to God.[3]

I would rather feel contrition than know its definition.

If you knew the whole Bible by heart, and the sayings of all the philosophers, what would this profit you without the love and grace of God?

"Vanity of vanities, all is vanity"—except to love God and to serve Him alone.[4]

This is the highest wisdom: to despise the world and to seek the kingdom of Heaven.[5]

4. It is therefore vanity to seek after the perishing riches, and to trust in them.[6]

It is also vanity to seek honors and to seek to climb to a high position.

It is vanity to follow the desires of the flesh and yearn for that which must bring with it grievous punishment.

It is vanity to desire to live long and not to care to live well.

It is vanity to be concerned only with this present life, and to make no provision for that which is to come.

It is vanity to love that which so speedily perishes and decays, and not to hasten on to where everlasting joy awaits you.

5. Call often to mind that proverb, "The eye is not satisfied with seeing, nor the ear with hearing."[7]

Endeavor then, to withdraw your heart from the love of visible things, and to turn yourself to that which is invisible.[8]

For they who follow their own sensual lusts defile their consciences and lose the grace of God.[9]

[1] *John 8:12*
[2] *Revelation 2:17*
[3] *Acts 10:35*
[4] *Eccl. 1:2, Deut. 6:13*
[5] *Matthew 6:33*
[6] *Matthew 6:19,20*
[7] *Ecclesiastes 1:8*
[8] *II Corinthians 4:18*
[9] *Heb. 12:15, II Pet. 2:10*

CHAPTER 2

On Thinking Humbly of Ourselves

All men naturally desire knowledge;[1] but what good is knowledge without the fear of God?

Surely a humble peasant who serves God is better than a proud philosopher who, neglecting his own soul, occupies himself in studying the course of the stars.

Whoever truly knows himself is lowly in his own eyes, and does not delight in the praises of men.

If I understood everything in the world and did not have divine love, what would it avail me in the sight of God, who will judge me according to my deeds?[2]

2. Give up that excessive desire for knowledge, for therein is to be found much distraction and deception.

Learned men are anxious to appear learned to others, and to be called wise.

There are many things the knowledge of which does little or no good to the soul.

And he is very unwise who sets his mind on anything more than he does on those things which aid him in his salvation.

Many words do not satisfy the soul, but a good life comforts the heart and a clean conscience gives great confidence toward God.[3]

3. The more you know and the better you understand, the more strictly you will be judged, unless your life is also more holy.

Do not be elated in your own mind, then, because of any ability or knowledge you may possess, but rather let the knowledge given you make you more humble and cautious.

If you think that you understand and know much, know also that there are many more things you do not know.

So do not be proud and puffed up with your knowledge,[4] but rather acknowledge your own ignorance.[5] Why would you set yourself above others, since there are many more learned and more skillful in the Scripture than you are?

If you would know or learn anything to your own good, then desire to be unknown and to be reputed as nothing.[6]

4. The highest and most profitable learning is a true knowledge and humble opinion of oneself.

It is great wisdom and perfection to think nothing of ourselves, and always to think well and highly of others.

If you should see another openly sin or commit some grievous offense, yet you should not think yourself better because of it; for you do not know how long you will be able to stand.

We are all weak and frail; but you should esteem no one more frail than yourself.

[1]Aristotle, *Metaphysics, I, 1.* [2]*Matthew 7:21, I Corinthians 13:2* [3]*I Timothy 3:9*
[4]*Romans 11:20* [5]*Romans 12:16*
[6]*Ama nesciri* (Love to be unknown) is quoted from St. Bernard. It was a favorite phrase among the Brethren of the Common Life. We are told that this entire sentence appears in another work of à Kempis, *The Little Alphabet of a Monk.*

Chapter 3

On the Teaching of Truth

Happy is the one whom Truth itself teaches, not by figures and words that pass away; but as it is in itself.[1]

Our own opinions and our own senses often deceive us, and they discern but little.

What good is it to argue and dispute much about obscure and hidden things–things we shall not be held to account for in the Day of Judgment?

It is great folly to neglect the things that are profitable and necessary, and deliberately to give our minds to dwell on curious and hurtful things. We have eyes and see not!

2. What do we have to do with such things as *genera* and *species*?[2] He to whom the Eternal Word speaks is delivered from a world of unnecessary opinions.

From that one Word all things proceed, and all things speak of Him. This is the Beginning, who also speaks to us.[3]

No one without that Word understands or judges rightly.

The person to whom all things are one, who reduces or returns all things to One, and looks at everything in One, may enjoy a quiet mind and remain at peace in God.[4]

O God, You are the Truth! Make me one with You in everlasting Love.

I am often wearied by reading and hearing many things: in You is all that I would have or can desire.

Let all the teachers hold their peace; let all creatures be silent in Your sight: let it be You alone, O Lord, who speaks to me.

3. The more one is unified within himself, becoming inwardly simple and uncomplicated, the more and higher

things he can understand without labor or effort, because he receives the light of wisdom from above.[5]

A pure, simple, and stable spirit is not distracted, even though it is busy in many works, because it does all for the glory of God, and being inwardly still and quiet, does not seek itself in any thing it does.

What hinders and troubles you more than the undisciplined passions of your own heart?

A good and godly man arranges in his mind beforehand those things which he is to do outwardly.

He does not allow them to draw him into any sort of sinful inclination, but orders them according to the rule of sound judgment.

Who has a greater battle than one who sets out to overcome himself?

This ought to be our endeavor: to conquer ourselves and daily to grow stronger against ourselves, and to grow in holiness.

4. All perfection in this life has mixed with it some measure of imperfection; and all our knowledge of ourselves has some darkness in it still.[6]

A humble knowledge of yourself is a surer way to God than a deep searching after learning.

Yet learning is not to be blamed, nor the mere knowledge of anything whatsoever to be despised, it being good in itself and ordained by God; but a good conscience and a godly life is always to be preferred before it.

But because many endeavor to get knowledge rather than to live well, they are often deceived and reap little or no benefit from their labor.

5. If only men bestowed as much labor in rooting out vices and planting virtues, as they do in raising controversial questions, there would neither be so much harm done

nor so great scandal given to the world, and there would not be such laxity in religious communities.

At the Day of Judgment we shall not be examined on what we have read, but what we have done; not on how well we have spoken, but on how faithfully we have lived.[7]

Tell me, where are all those Doctors and Masters with whom you were so well acquainted while they lived and flourished in learning?

Others now fill their places and perhaps scarcely ever think of those who went before them. In their lifetime they were thought to be something, but now they are not even mentioned.

6. How quickly does the glory of the world pass away![8] Would that their life had agreed well with their knowledge! Then they would have studied and read to a good purpose.

How many perish by reason of vain learning of this world[9] who pay little attention to the serving of God.

And because they choose to be great rather than humble, they become vain in their imaginations.[10]

He is truly great who has great love.

He is truly great who is little in his own eyes and counts as nothing the very highest of honors.[11]

He is truly wise who accounts all earthly things as refuse, that he might win Christ.[12]

He is truly learned who does the will of God and abandons his own will.

[1]*Psalm 94:12* [2]Philosophical disputes current when this was written.
[3]*John 1:1* [4]*Isaiah 26:3, I Cor. 2:2* [5]*Matthew 11:25, James 3:17*
[6]*I Cor. 13:12* [7]*Matthew 7:21, 22*
[8]*O quam cito transit gloria mundi.* The usual form was *sic transit gloria mundi,* and these words are addressed to the Pope on the occasion of his elevation.
[9]*Titus 1:10* [10]*Romans 1:21* [11]*Matthew 18:4, 23:11*
[12]*Philippians 3:8*

Chapter 4

On Wisdom and Forethought in Our Actions

We must not believe every saying or suggestion, but we should carefully and patiently ponder all things in relation to the will of God.

But alas! Such is our weakness that we would often rather believe and speak evil of others than good.

But perfect men do not easily give credence to everything anyone tells them, for they know that human nature is prone to evil and words are easily misused.[1]

2. It is great wisdom not to proceed over-hastily in anything, nor to hold stubbornly to your own opinions.[2]

Also, it is wise not to believe everything you hear, nor to be hasty in repeating to others what you have heard or believe.[3]

Consult with someone who is wise and conscientious and seek to be instructed by one better than yourself, rather than to follow your own inclinations and opinions.

A good life makes one wise according to God, and gives him experience in many things.[4]

The more lowly a man is in his own eyes and the more obedient he is to God, so much more wise will he be in all his affairs, and the more he will enjoy peace and quietness of heart.

[1]*Genesis 8:21, James 3:2* [2]*Proverbs 19:2* [3]*Proverbs 17:9*
[4]*Proverbs 15:33, Eccl. 1:16*

CHAPTER 5

On Reading the Holy Scriptures

Truth, not eloquence, is to be sought in Holy Scripture. Each part of the Scripture must be read with the same Spirit by which it was written.

We should seek our spiritual profit in the Scripture rather than looking for subtle arguments.

We should read those books that are simple and devout as well as those that are lofty and profound.

Do not let the ignorance of the writer concern you, whether he be of small or great learning, but let the love of simple truth draw you to read. Do not ask who wrote this or that, but take heed to what is spoken.

2. Men pass away, but the "truth of the Lord endures forever."[1] God speaks to us in many ways without respect of persons.[2]

Our own curiosity often hinders us in the reading of Scripture, for we stop to examine and discuss that which we should pass over and accept.

If you desire to benefit, read with humility, simplicity, and faith, and never desire to make yourself appear learned.

Ask freely, and hear with silence the words of holy men. Do not let the parables of the Fathers displease you, for they are not told without good cause.[3]

[1]*Psalm 117:2* [2]*Romans 2:11, Hebrews 1:1* [3]*Proverbs 1:6, Ecclesiastes 12:9*

Chapter 6

On Inordinate Affections

Whenever a man desires anything inordinately,[1] he is at once disquieted within himself.

The proud and covetous can never rest. The poor and humble in spirit dwell in the multitude of peace.

The man who is not completely dead to himself is quickly tempted and overcome in small and trifling things.

The weak in spirit, and he who is as yet in bondage to carnal and material things, can only draw himself from worldly desires with great difficulty.

Therefore, he is often afflicted and sad when he sets about to withdraw himself from them and is quickly angered when any opposition comes against him.

2. If he has given in to his lusts and obtained what he desired, he is soon plagued with remorse of conscience, because he yielded to his passion and thus robbed himself of the very peace he sought.

True quietness of heart, therefore, is achieved by resisting our passions, not by obeying them.

There is no peace in the heart of a carnal man, nor of one who is wholly given up to outward things; but in a fervent, spiritual man who has his delight in God is found great peace and inward quietness.

[1] *Inordinate:* not kept within bounds, immoderate, unrestrained, excessive. It implies the exceeding of bounds prescribed by authority or dictated by good judgment. It appears often in this work, but is not a word in common use for many Christians today.

Chapter 7

On Avoiding Vain Hope and Pride

He is foolish indeed who puts his trust in man or in any creature.

Do not be ashamed to serve others for the love of Jesus Christ and to be considered poor in this world.

Do not presume to trust yourself, but place your hope in God.[1]

Do what is in your power to do, and God will honor your heart's intent.

Do not trust in your own knowledge,[2] nor in the cleverness of any living soul, but rather in the grace of God, who helps the humble and humbles the proud.[3]

2. If you have wealth, do not glory in it, nor in your powerful friends. Rather glory in God who gives all things and who, above all, desires to give you Himself.

Do not pride yourself because of your physical stature or your beauty, which may be marred or destroyed by a small illness.

Do not take pleasure in your natural gifts or your readiness of wit, lest you offend God, who created all the good whatever that you have received by nature.

3. Do not consider yourself better than others, lest perhaps in the sight of God, who knows what is in man, you be accounted worse than they.

Do not be proud in well-doing, for the judgment of God is far different from the judgment of men, and He is often offended by that which men find pleasing.

If there is any good in you, you should believe that there is much more in others, and so preserve your humility.

It does you no harm to consider yourself worse than all men, but it does you great harm to exalt yourself above even one.

The humble enjoy continual peace, but the heart of the proud is full of jealousy and frequent indignation.

[1]*Psalm 31:1* [2]*Jeremiah 9:23* [3]*James 4:6*

CHAPTER 8

On Shunning Too Much Familiarity

Do not lay open your heart to everyone, but in all your affairs, seek the counsel of those who are wise and who fear God.

Do not talk much with the young nor with strangers.

Do not flatter the rich, nor seek the presence of great and famous people.

Keep company with the simple and humble, with the devout and upright. Talk with them on those things which will edify. Do not be familiar with any woman, but in general commend all good women to God.

Desire to have close fellowship with God alone and with His holy angels, and avoid the acquaintance of men as much as you may.

2. We must have charity towards all, but familiarity with all is not expedient.

Sometimes it happens that a person unknown to us is highly commended by the good reports of others, but he turns out to be offensive on closer contact.

We think sometimes that we please others by our presence when in fact we are offensive to them by those bad qualities which they can see in us.

Chapter 9

On Obedience and Subjection

It is a very great thing to live in obedience, to be under a superior, and not to be free to do as we please.

It is much safer to obey than to govern.

Many live under obedience more from necessity than from love, and such are discontented and easily complain. They cannot attain freedom of mind unless they willingly and heartily put themselves under obedience for the love of God.

Go wherever you will, but you will still find no rest except in humble subjection under the government of a superior. Many have deceived themselves, imagining they would find happiness in change.

2. It is true that everyone readily does that which most agrees with his own liking, and is most drawn to those who are like-minded.

But if God is among us, we must sometimes for the sake of peace let go of our own opinions.

Who is so wise that he can fully know all things?

Do not, therefore, be too confident in your own opinion, but be willing to hear the judgment of others.

If what you think is really sound and yet you give it up for God and follow the opinion of another, it will be turned to your greater good.

3. I have often heard that it is safer to hear and take counsel than to give it.

It may also happen that each one's opinion may be good; but to refuse to yield to others when reason or special cause require it, is a mark of pride and obstinacy.

Chapter 10

On Avoiding Too Much Talk

Avoid the tumult of the world as much as possible, because talk of worldly affairs is a great hindrance, even though it be done with good intentions.

For we are quickly deceived and captured by vanity.

Oftentimes I could wish I had held my peace when I have spoken, and that I had not been in the company of others.

Why do we so eagerly speak and talk with one another when we so seldom return to silence without hurt to our conscience?

The reason is that we seek comfort from one another in such talk and want to ease our mind, overburdened with our many thoughts.

We very eagerly talk and think of those things we most love or desire, or of the things we dislike most.

2. But alas! It is often in vain and to no good, because the outward satisfaction of our talk caused us no small loss of inward and divine consolation.

Therefore we must watch and pray, so that our time will not pass away idly.

If it is permissible and expedient for you to talk, speak of those things that may edify.

Evil habits and neglect of our own growth in grace are

the chief causes of our thoughtless and idle talk.

Yet talking of spiritual things greatly aids our spiritual growth, especially when persons of one mind and spirit are gathered together in God.

CHAPTER 11

On Attaining Peace and the Desire for Growth in Grace

We would enjoy much peace if we did not occupy ourselves with the words and activities of others, and with things that are of no concern to us.[1]

How can he remain long in peace who intrudes himself into the cares of others, who seeks occasions to travel about, and who seldom gives serious thought to himself?

Blessed are the single-hearted, for they shall enjoy much peace.[2]

2. Why were many of the saints so perfect and contemplative?

Because they labored to die wholly to all earthly desires, and therefore they could with their whole heart cleave to God and give themselves wholly to Him.

We are led too much by our feelings and we are too concerned about transitory things.

We seldom overcome even one fault perfectly; we have too little zeal to grow spiritually every day, and so we remain cold and lukewarm.

3. If we were perfectly dead to ourselves, and not entangled with outward things, we would be able to taste and

relish spiritual things, and to have some experience of heavenly contemplation.

The greatest, and indeed the only hindrance, is that we are not free from passions and lusts, nor do we attempt to walk in the perfect way of the saints. When some small difficulty arises, we are quickly dejected and turn to people for consolation.

4. If we tried like brave men to stand in this spiritual battle, surely we would experience the help of God from Heaven.

He who gives us the occasion to fight to the end that we may obtain the victory is ready to help those who fight, trusting in His grace.[3]

If we rely only on some outward observances for progress in our spiritual life, our devotion will quickly run out.

But let us lay the axe to the root, so that being freed from our passions, we may find rest to our souls.

5. If we would root out one fault every year, we would soon become mature.

But as it is now, we often notice, on the contrary, that we were better and purer at the beginning of our conversion than after many years of our profession.

Our fervor and our progress should increase daily; but it is now considered a great thing if a man can retain even some part of his initial zeal.

If we would do but a little violence against ourselves at the beginning, we would be able to perform everything with ease and delight.

6. It is a hard matter to give up evil habits, but it is even harder to go against our own will.

If you cannot overcome the small and easy things, how will you overcome the harder ones?

Resist your evil inclinations at the very start, and break evil habits, lest they pull you little by little into even greater trouble.

If you only knew how much inward peace to yourself and joy to others your good demeanor would obtain, I think you would take more care about your spiritual growth.

[1]*Psalm 131:1, 2* [2]*Matthew 5:8* [3]*I Corinthians 10:13*

Chapter 12

On Profiting from Adversities

It is good that we sometimes have troubles and crosses, for they often make a man think about himself, and consider that he is here in a state of exile and ought not to place his trust in any worldly thing.

It is good that we are sometimes opposed, and that others think ill of us or misunderstand us, even though we have done and intended well.

These things often help us to attain humility and defend us from vain glory, for we are more inclined to seek God for our inward witness when we are outwardly scorned by others and no credit is given us.

2. A man should therefore so settle himself in God that he does not rely on the reassurances of man.

When a godly man is afflicted, tempted, or troubled with evil thoughts, then he understands better the great need he has for God, and he knows then that he can do nothing good without Him.

Then he grieves and laments and turns to prayer because of the miseries he is suffering.[1]

He is weary of living and even longs for death to release him that he might depart and be with Christ.[2]

Then he understands well that perfect security and peace cannot be found in this world.[3]

[1]*II Corinthians 7:9* [2]*Philippians 1:23, II Corinthians 1:8* [3]*John 16:33*

Chapter 13

On Resisting Temptation

As long as we live in this world we cannot avoid trial and temptation.

It is written in Job, "The life of man on earth is a warfare."[1]

Everyone should, therefore, be careful about his temptations, watching in prayer lest the devil find an opportunity to deceive him; for he never sleeps, but goes about seeking whom he may devour.[2]

No man is so perfect and holy that he does not experience temptations at times, and we cannot be altogether without them.

2. Nevertheless temptations are often very profitable to us, even though they are troublesome and grievous, for in them a man is humbled, purified, and taught.[3]

All the saints passed through many trials and temptations and profited by them.[4]

But they who could not bear temptations became reprobate and fell away.

There is no Order so holy nor place so secret that there are no temptations or adversities in it.

3. There is no man who is altogether free from temptations while he lives on this earth, because the root of temptation is in ourselves, who are born with an inclination to evil.[5]

When one temptation or trial goes away, another comes; we shall always have something to suffer, because we are fallen from the state of our original happiness.

Many seek to avoid temptations and fall even more grievously into them.

By flight alone we cannot conquer, but by patience and humility we become stronger than all our enemies.

He who avoids temptations outwardly and does not pull them up by the roots shall benefit but little. Indeed, temptations will the sooner return to him and will be more violent than before.

Little by little, by patience and perseverance through God's help, you will overcome more easily than by violence and by your own annoyance.

Seek counsel often in temptation and do not deal harshly with one who is tempted, but encourage and strengthen him as you would desire for yourself.

4. The beginning of all temptations is double-mindedness and too little confidence in God.[6]

For as a ship without a helm is tossed to and fro by the waves, so is the man tempted in many ways who is careless and gives up his purposes.[7]

Fire tries iron, and temptation proves the righteous man.

We often do not know what we are able to do until temptations show us what we are.

Yet we must be watchful, especially at the beginning of a temptation, for the enemy is then more easily overcome if he is not allowed to enter the door of our hearts, but is resisted at the very gate on his first knock.

For this reason it has been said, "Withstand the beginnings! The remedy is applied too late when the evil has grown strong through long delay."[8]

For first there comes to the mind a bare thought of evil, then a strong imagination of it, and then delight and a strong urge to evil, and then consent.

Thus, little by little our wicked enemy gains complete entrance because he was not resisted at the very start.

And the longer a man is negligent in resisting, the weaker he becomes, and the stronger the enemy becomes against him.

5. Some experience great temptations at the beginning of their conversion, while others in the end.

Still others are much troubled almost through their whole life.

Some are but slightly tempted. All this is in accordance with the wisdom and justice of God's ordinance, who weighs the states and merit of men, and orders everything for the welfare of His own elect.

6. We should not, therefore, despair when we are tempted, but should pray all the more fervently to God that He will vouchsafe to help us in all our trials; for He will surely, as St. Paul tells us, make with every temptation a way of escape, that we will be able to bear it.[9]

7. Temptations and afflictions prove how much a man has progressed; and his reward is thereby increased and his virtues are more plainly manifest.

It is no great thing for a man to be fervent and devout when he feels no affliction, but if in the time of adversity he bears himself patiently, there is hope then of great growth in grace.

Some are kept from great temptations and yet are often overcome in the daily small ones, so that, being humbled, they may never presume on themselves in great matters, seeing that they are defeated in such small ones.

[1]*Job 7:1, Latin Version* [2]*I Peter 5:8* [3]*James 1:2*
[4]*Acts 14:22* [5]*James 1:14* [6]*James 1:7*
[7]*James 1:16* [8]*Ovid, Of Remedies, Bk. XIII* [9]*I Corinthians 10:13*

CHAPTER 14

On Avoiding Rash Judgments

Look to yourself and do not judge the deeds of others.[1] In judging others, a man labors in vain, is often in error, and easily falls into sin.[2] But in judging and examining himself, he always labors fruitfully.

We often judge things by our personal feelings, and our selfish motives easily rob us of right judgment.

If God were always the true object of our desire, we would not be troubled so easily when our opinions are disputed.

2. But often something within or some outward occurrence draws us after it.

Many unknowingly serve themselves in what they do.

They seem to live in good peace of mind as long as things are done according to their will or opinion, but if things happen otherwise than as they desire, they are immediately sad and upset.

Diversities of judgments and opinions are often the cause of dissension between friends and neighbors, even between religious and devout persons.[3]

3. An old custom is hard to break, and no man is easily led farther than he himself can see.[4]

If you rely more on your own reasoning and effort than upon obedience to Jesus Christ, it will be a long time before you are truly enlightened. This is because God will have us completely subject and obedient to Himself, that being inflamed with His love, we may rise above the narrow limits of our human reason.

[1]*Matthew 7:1, Romans 15:1* [2]*Ecclesiastes 3:16* [3]*Matthew 12:25, Luke 12:51* [4]*Jeremiah 13:23*

Chapter 15

On Works of Love

Do no evil thing for cause in the world, nor for the love of any human being; yet, for the welfare of one who is in need, a good work may sometimes be interrupted without any scruple, or even exchanged for a better one.[1]

By doing this, a good work is not lost, but changed into a better.

Without love, the outward work avails nothing; but whatever is done in love, though it may be ever so small and contemptible in the sight of the world, is wholly fruitful.[2]

For God considers more the measure of love with which a man works than the measure of the deed. He does much who loves much.[3]

2. He does much who does a thing well. He does well who serves the common good rather than his own will.[4]

Oftentimes a work may appear to be done out of love which is instead a work of the flesh, because some natural inclination, self-will, hope of reward, and our own self-interest are motives seldom absent.

3. He who has true and perfect love seeks himself in nothing, but only desires in all things that the glory of God should be exalted.[5]

He also envies no one, because he seeks nothing for self; neither does he choose to rejoice in himself, but desires above all things to be made happy in the enjoyment of God.[6]

He attributes nothing that is good to any man, but refers it entirely to God, from whom, as from a fountain, all things proceed, and in whom all the saints finally rest as in their highest fulfillment.

If a man had in his heart but one spark of true love, he would certainly discern that all earthly things are full of vanity.

[1]*Matthew 18:8* [2]*I Corinthians 13:3* [3]*Luke 7:47*
[4]*Philippians 2:17* [5]*Philippians 2:21, I Corinthians 13:5* [6]*Psalms 17:15, 24:6*

Chapter 16

On Bearing with the Faults of Others

Those things that a man cannot change in himself or in others, he should patiently endure until God orders them otherwise.

Think that it is perhaps better thus for our trial and patience, without which all our good deeds are worth little.

You should, of course, pray when you have such infirmities that God will vouchsafe to help you, and that you may bear them rightly.[1]

2. If one who is warned once or twice will not be corrected, do not contend with him, but commit all to God that His will may be done,[2] and His Name honored in all

His servants. For well He knows how to turn evil into good.[3]

Try to be patient in bearing with the defects and infirmities of others, whatever they may be. Remember that you also have many failings which others must bear.[4]

If you cannot make yourself what you would like to be, how can you expect to have anyone else exactly as you would like them?[5]

We would willingly have others perfect, and yet we do not amend our own faults.

3. We would have others severely corrected and would not be corrected ourselves.

The great freedom of others offends us, and yet we do not want to have our own desires denied us.

We would have others kept under by strict laws, but in no sort would we be restrained ourselves.

And thus it appears, how seldom we weigh ourselves and our neighbors on the same scale.

If all men were perfect, what then would we have to suffer in our neighbor for the love of God?

4. But God has so ordered it, that we may learn to bear one another's burdens; for no man is without fault, no man without his burden. No man is sufficient of himself, or wise enough of himself. But we ought to bear with one another, comfort one another, help, instruct, and admonish one another.[6]

Occasions of adversity best show the measure of virtue or strength each one has.

For such occasions do not make a man weak, but reveal what he already is.

[1]*Matt. 6:13, Luke 11:4* [2]*Matt. 6:10* [3]*Genesis 50:20*
[4]*Galatians 6:1* [5]*I Thess. 5:14* [6]*Gal. 6:2, I Cor. 12:25*

Chapter 17

On Life in a Religious Community

You must learn to submit your own will in many things if you would live in peace and harmony with others.

It is not an easy thing to live in a religious community or monastery, to persevere in it faithfully even unto death.

Blessed is he who has lived there well and happily to the end. If you would be stable and grow in grace as you should, consider yourself a pilgrim and stranger on earth.[1]

You must be contented for Christ's sake to be counted a fool in this world, if you desire to live the life of a Religious.[2]

Dress and tonsure amount to little. What makes a true Religious is a change of heart and complete putting to death of the carnal passions.

He who seeks anything but God alone and the salvation of his soul will find nothing but trials and grief.

He cannot remain long in peace who does not labor to be the least and subject to all.[3]

You came to serve, not to rule.[4] Know that you were called to suffer and labor, not to be idle nor to spend your time in idle chatter.

Here men are tried as gold in the furnace.

Here no man can abide unless he is ready to humble himself with his whole heart for the love of God.

[1]*I Peter 2:11, Hebrews 11:13* [2]*I Corinthians 4:10* [3]*Luke 22:26* [4]*Matthew 20:26*

Chapter 18

On the Examples of the Holy Fathers

Consider the lively examples of the holy Fathers, in whom true perfection and godliness shone, and you will see that in the present time we do little or nothing by comparison.[1]

Alas! What is our life when we are compared with them!

The saints and friends of Christ served the Lord in hunger and thirst, in cold and nakedness, in labor and weariness, in watchings and fastings, in prayer and meditation, in many persecutions and reproaches.

2. Oh, how numerous and grievous the trials which were suffered by the apostles, martyrs, confessors, virgins, and all those who endeavored to follow Christ! For they hated their lives in this world that they might keep them to eternal life.[2]

How strict and self-renouncing a life did those Fathers in the desert lead! What grievous temptations they suffered! How often were they fiercely assailed by their spiritual enemies, and what frequent and fervent prayer did they offer to God![3]

What rigorous abstinences did they use, and how great zeal and care did they show for their spiritual growth! How strong a battle did they fight in overcoming their lusts! What singlehearted and pure intent did they keep towards God![4]

In the day they labored, and in the night they prayed. And even as they labored during the day, they did not cease from mental prayer.[5]

3. They spent their whole time profitably; every hour seemed short in the service of God; and through the great

sweetness they felt in contemplation, even the need of bodily refreshment was forgotten.

They renounced all riches, dignities, honors, friends, and relatives; they desired nothing from this world; they ate the bare necessities of life, and begrudged even the necessary care of the body.[6]

They were poor in things of this world but very rich in grace and virtue.[7]

Outwardly they were destitute, but inwardly they were refreshed with grace and divine consolation.

4. They were strangers to the world, but near and familiar friends to God.[8]

They considered themselves to be nothing, and to this present world they seemed despicable; but they were precious and beloved in the sight of God.[9]

Grounded in true humility, they lived in simple obedience and walked in love and patience. Therefore they grew daily in the Spirit and obtained great grace in God's sight.

They were given as an example to all Religious persons, and they should provoke us more to endeavor for our own spiritual advancement than the example of the lukewarm entice us to grow slack.

5. How great was their devotion to prayer! What ambition to excel others in virtue! What exact discipline then flourished! What respect and obedience to the rule of their Superior flourished in them all!

Truly their deeds yet bear witness that they were holy and perfect, and so mightily subdued the world and thrust it underfoot.

But nowadays anyone who does not violate the rules and who can with patience keep even some little spark of the virtue and fervor he had at the beginning is accounted great!

6. But alas for sorrow! It is through our own apathy and negligence in these times that we fall so quickly from our initial enthusiasm into such weakness and lukewarmness of spirit, making our life in truth very tedious to us.

Would to God that the desire to grow in grace not remain asleep in you, who have often seen the many examples of holy lives!

[1]*Heb. 11:38, I Cor. 4:11* [2]*Luke 14:26* [3]*II Corinthians 11:25, 26*
[4]*I Corinthians 9:27* [5]*I Thessalonians 5:17* [6]*Revelation 12:11*
[7]*Matthew 5:3, Luke 6:20* [8]*Exodus 33:11* [9]*Psalm 116:15*

Chapter 19

On the Exercises of a Good Religious

The life of a good Religious[1] should shine in all virtues, so that he may inwardly be what he outwardly appears to others.

Indeed, there ought to be much more within than appears outwardly, for God sees us, to whom we are bound to give highest reverence wherever we may be, and in whose sight we are to walk in purity as do the angels.

We should renew our purpose daily, and should stir up ourselves to fresh enthusiasm, as though this were the first day of our conversion, and we should say, "Help me, Lord Jesus, that I may persevere in my good purpose and in Your holy service to my life's end. Grant that I may now, this very day, perfectly begin, for what I have done in time past is as nothing."

2. According to our purpose, so shall be our spiritual advancement, and much diligence is necessary for one who would make much progress.

If even one with a firm purpose fail often, what will one do who only seldom or weakly ever resolves anything?

Yet in various ways we do forsake our purpose, and even a slight omission of our spiritual exercises brings loss to our souls.

The resolve of righteous men does not depend on their own wisdom, but on God's grace, on which they always rely for whatever they undertake.

For man proposes, but God disposes; neither is the way of man in himself.[2]

3. If an accustomed exercise is sometimes omitted either for some act of piety or to help our brother, it may easily be recovered again later on.

But if, out of weariness or carelessness we lightly omit it, it is reprehensible indeed and will be hurtful to our souls. Even doing the best we can, we shall still all too easily fail in many things.[3]

Yet we must always have a steady resolution, especially against those sins which hinder us most.

We must diligently inquire into and set in order both our outward and inward life, because both are important to our growth in godliness.

4. If you cannot continually collect yourself, do it sometimes, at least twice a day, morning and night.

In the morning fix your good resolves, and at night examine yourself as to how you have done, how you have acted in word, deed, and thought, for in these you may have often offended both God and your neighbor.[4]

Gird up your loins like a man against the vile assaults of the devil; curb your appetite and you will better be able to subdue all the unruly passions of the flesh.[5]

Never be entirely idle, but either be reading, writing, praying, or meditating, or doing something for the common good.[6]

As for bodily exercises, they must be used with discretion, but they are not to be practiced by all men alike.

5. Those devotions which do not belong to the entire community should not be done openly, for private devotions are most safely practiced in secret.

Nevertheless you must be careful not to neglect the public devotions in favor of private ones. But having done fully and faithfully all that is required of you, if you still have any spare time, then in privacy give yourself to devotion as you feel inclined.

Everyone cannot use the same kind of spiritual exercise, but one is more useful for this person, another for that.

Different exercises are also suited to varying circumstances; some are better on working days, others on holy days.

We need one kind in the time of temptation, and others in times of peace and quietness.

Some better suit us when we are pensive, others when we are joyful in the Lord.

6. About the time of the great festivals, good exercises should be renewed and the prayers of the saints more fervently sought.

We ought to make our resolutions from one feast to another, as though we were then to depart from this world and come to the eternal feast in Heaven.

We ought carefully to prepare ourselves at holy seasons to live more devoutly and to keep stricter watch on all things that we are to observe, as though we were shortly to receive the reward of our labors from God's own hand.[7]

7. If our reward is deferred, let us assume that we are not sufficiently prepared and are yet unworthy of that great glory which shall be revealed in us[8] in due time, and let us endeavor to prepare ourselves better for our departure.

"Blessed is the servant," says St. Luke, "whom his Lord when He comes shall find watching. Verily I say to you, He shall make him ruler over all His possessions."[9]

[1]The word *Religious* refers to a member of a monastery or religious community.
[2]*Proverbs 16:9* [3]*Ecclesiastes 7:20* [4]*Psalms 5:3, 139:23, 24*
[5]*Ephesians 6:11* [6]*II Thessalonians 3:13* [7]*I Thessalonians 5:2*
[8]*Romans 8:18* [9]*Luke 12:43, 44*

Chapter 20

On the Love of Solitude and Silence

Seek a convenient time to search your own conscience and think often on the loving kindness of God.

Do not read for curiosity's sake or simply to fill up the time, but read such things as will stir your heart to devotion.

If you will refrain from idle talk and idly running about, from listening to gossip and rumors, you will find ample time for meditation on good things.

The most holy men and women who ever lived avoided the company of worldly men whenever they could, and chose rather to live with God in the secret of their own hearts.

2. One holy man said, "As often as I have been among worldly company, I have departed less a man than I was before."[1]

And this we know well when we talk long together, for it is easier not to speak at all, than to speak without overtalking.

It is easier to stay alone at home than to keep due watch over ourselves in company.

Therefore he who intends to reach that which is inward and spiritual must go with Jesus "apart from the multitude."[2]

No one can safely appear among the people but he who would choose to remain alone if he might.

No one can safely speak but he who would gladly be silent.

No one can safely be in charge but he who is glad to be under others.

No one can safely command but he who has learned to obey.[3]

3. No man can truly rejoice but he whose heart witnesses that he has a clean conscience.[4]

And yet the security of the saints was always in weakness and in the fear of God.

And though such blessed men shined in all virtue, yet they were not therefore swelled up in pride, but were even more diligent in the service of God and humble in all their doings.

But the boldness of wicked men comes out of their pride and presumption, and in the end it deceives them.

Although you seem to be a good Religious or a devout solitary, do not promise yourself security in this life.[5]

4. Often those who stand in the highest esteem of men have fallen more grievously because of their over-confidence.

It is more profitable to many that they should not be altogether free from temptations, but should be assaulted frequently, lest they should feel over-confident and become puffed up with pride, or should lean too freely on worldly comforts.

How good a conscience would he keep who never sought after fleeting pleasure or entangled himself with the world!

If a man would cut off all vain worry, thinking only of spiritual things which are profitable to the soul, and place all his hope in God, what great peace and quietness he would possess![6]

5. No man is worthy of heavenly comfort unless he has diligently exercised himself in holy contrition.

If you desire true contrition of heart, enter your secret chamber, and shut out the tumults of the world, as it is written, "Commune with your own heart on your bed and be still."[7] In your cell you will find what you often lose outside it.

The more you dwell in your cell, the more you will enjoy it; the less you come to it, the more you will loathe it. If in the beginning of your conversion you are content to remain in it and keep it well, it will become to you a dear friend and a most pleasant solace.

6. In silence and in stillness the devout soul advances and learns the mysteries of the Holy Scriptures.

There the soul finds rivers of tears wherein she may every night wash and cleanse herself. The more she withdraws from the distraction of the world, the more familiar can she become with her Creator.

Whoever then withdraws himself from acquaintances and friends, God will draw near him with His holy angels.

It is better for a man to be unknown and to take heed for his own soul than to work miracles in the world.

It is praiseworthy for a Religious to go abroad but seldom, and to have no desire to see or be seen.

7. Why would you long to see that which it is unlawful for you to have? The world passes away with its lusts.[8]

The lusts of the flesh draw you abroad, but when the time is past, what do you bring home with you but a burdened conscience and a distracted heart?

A merry going forth often brings a mournful return, and a jolly night often makes a sad morning.[9]

So all carnal pleasures enter gently, but in the end they bite and sting to death. [10]

What can you see elsewhere that you cannot see here? Behold the heavens and the earth and all the elements, for out of these all things were created.

8. What can you see anywhere that can last long under the sun?

You think that perhaps you will be able to satisfy yourself, but you cannot.

Even if you could see everything that exists in front of your eyes, what would that be but a vain sight?

Lift up your eyes to God on high, and ask Him to forgive your sins and negligences.

Leave vain things to vain men, and be intent on those things which God has commanded you.

Close the door behind you and call to yourself Jesus your Beloved.[11]

9. Remain with Him in your closet, for you will never find such great peace anywhere else.

If you had not gone abroad or listened to idle talk, you would have better kept a happy peace of mind. But since you sometimes delight to hear new things, it is only right that you should suffer some disquietude of heart.

[1]Seneca, *Ep. VII*
[2]*John 5:13*
[3]*Ecclesiastes 2:7-11*
[4]*II Corinthians 1:12*
[5]*Phillipians 3:13*
[6]*Isaiah 26:3*
[7]*Psalm 4:4*
[8]*I John 2:17*
[9]*Proverbs 14:13*
[10]*Proverbs 14:12*
[11]*Matthew 6:6*

Chapter 21

On Contrition of Heart

If you would make any progress in godliness, keep yourself in the fear of God and do not seek too much freedom. Restrain all your passions under discipline and do not give yourself to foolish mirth.[1]

Give yourself rather to contrition[2] of heart and you will gain much in devotion by it.

Contrition opens the way to much good which laxness quickly destroys.

It is a wonder that any man can ever heartily rejoice in this life if he weighs and duly considers the state of his exile and the many dangers surrounding his soul.

2. Levity of heart and small attention to our faults prevent us from feeling the real sorrows of our souls; and we often laugh vainly when we have good cause to weep.

There is no true freedom or real joy but in the fear of God accompanied by a good conscience.

He is happy who can throw off all distracting hindrances and bring himself to the one single purpose of contrition.

Happy is he who can abandon whatever may stain or burden his conscience.

Fight manfully, for one habit overcomes another.

If you will let others alone in their affairs, they will likewise not hinder you in yours.

3. Do not busy yourself in affairs of others, and do not entangle yourself with the business of your superiors.

Keep your eye on yourself first of all and always correct yourself before all your friends.

If you do not have men's favor, do not let this grieve you;

but take this to heart, that you do not conduct yourself as carefully and circumspectly as becomes the servant of God or a devout Religious.[3]

It is often better and safer for a man not to have many comforts in this life, especially those of the flesh.[4]

If we very seldom or never taste divine consolations, the fault is ours, because we have not sought contrition of heart and have not utterly forsaken the vain and outward comforts of the world.

4. Acknowledge that you are unworthy of divine consolation and that you rather deserve much tribulation.

When a man has perfect contrition, then all the world seems grievous and bitter to him.[5]

A good man always finds sufficient cause for mourning and weeping.

For whether he considers himself or his neighbor's circumstance, he knows that none lives without tribulation.

And the more closely a man looks into himself, so much the more he sorrows.[7]

Our sins and wickednesses in which we lie so entangled that we can seldom contemplate heavenly things give us good reason for sorrow and inward contrition.[8]

5. If you thought more often of your death, rather than the length of life, you would doubtless be more zealous to change.[9]

If you seriously considered the torments of the other world, I believe you would be willing to endure any toil or sorrow in this world and would not be afraid to undergo any kind of hardship.[10]

But because these things do not enter our thoughts, we remain spiritually cold and indifferent, still loving only the things that please us.

6. It is often our lack of spirituality which makes our miserable body rebel so easily.

Pray humbly to the Lord then, that He will give you the spirit of contrition, and say in the words of the prophet, "Feed me, O Lord, with the bread of tears and give me abundance of tears to drink."[11]

[1]*Proverbs 19.3* [2]*Contrition* implies deep sorrow and desire to change.
[3]*Galatians 1:10* [4]*Psalm 76:5* [5]*Psalm 69:20*
[6]*Psalm 34:19* [7]*Psalm 69:5* [8]*Psalm 51:17*
[9]*Ecclesiastes 7:2* [10]*Matthew 25:41* [11]*Psalm 80:5*

Chapter 22

On the Consideration of Human Misery

Wherever you are and whenever you turn, you are miserable unless you turn to God.

Why are you troubled when things do not turn out as you would have them? Who is he who has everything to his liking? Neither you, nor I, nor any man on earth![1]

There is no one in this world, be he king or pope, free from trouble or perplexity.

Who then is better off? Surely, he who is able to suffer something for the love of God.

2. Many weak and foolish people say, "Look what a happy life so-and-so leads–how wealthy, how great he is, how powerful and famous!"[2]

But lift up your eyes to the riches of Heaven and you can see that all the good things of this life are nothing. They are all very uncertain and burdensome, because they are never possessed without some anxiety and fear.

Man's happiness does not consist in the abundance of

temporal goods; but a moderate portion is sufficient for him.[3]

It is truly a misery even to live on this earth.

The more a man desires to be spiritual, the more bitter this present life becomes to him, because he sees more clearly and understands more keenly the defects of human corruption.

To eat and drink, to sleep and watch, to rest, to labor, and to be subject to the other necessities of nature is truly a great misery and affliction to the godly man who would gladly be freed from all sin.[4]

3. For the inner life is weighed down in this world by the necessities of the body.

Therefore the psalmist prays fervently to be freed from them, saying, "Bring me out of my distresses."[5]

But woe to those who do not realize their own misery! And yet greater woe to those who love this miserable and corruptible life![6]

For there are some who so cling to it, that although they are scarcely able to get the necessities by work or by begging, yet if they could live here forever, they would care nothing for the kingdom of God.

4. How foolish and unbelieving in heart are these men, who lie so deeply buried in worldly things that they can relish nothing but carnal things!

But, miserable as they are, they will in the end feel to their loss how vile and vain was that which they loved.

On the other hand, the saints of God and all the loyal friends of Christ did not set their hearts on those things which pleased the flesh or were highly esteemed in this life, but rather with all their hope and their earnest endeavor, they aspired to the things which are above.[7]

Their whole desire was raised upward to things imperishable and invisible, so the desire for visible things could not draw them to things below.[8]

5. O my brother, do not throw away your desire of progressing in godliness; there is yet time, the hour is not past![9]

Why then procrastinate in your good resolution? Arise and begin this very instant, and say, "Now is the time to act, now is the time to fight, now is the proper time to change!"

When you are ill at ease and much troubled, then is the time to earn your reward.

You must pass through fire and water before you come into a spacious place.[10]

Unless you do violence to yourself, you will never overcome your vices.

As long as we have this frail body of ours, we can never be without sin or live without weariness and sorrow.

We would gladly have relief from all misery, but since we lost our innocence through sin, we have also lost our true happiness.

Therefore we must have patience and wait for the mercy of God till this tyranny be past and mortality is swallowed up by life.[11]

6. How great is human frailty, which is always prone to evil![12]

Today you confess a sin, and tomorrow you commit the very same sin you confessed!

Now you resolve to look well to your ways, and within an hour you act as though you had resolved nothing at all.

We have good cause, then, to humble ourselves and never to think highly of ourselves, since we are so frail and unstable.

By our own negligence we may quickly lose that which by much labor through the grace of God was hardly attained.

7. What will become of us in the end, who begin to grow lukewarm so soon?

Woe to us if we choose to rest as though all were now peace and safety, when as yet there appears no sign of true holiness in our lives.[13]

We need to begin afresh like young novices to be taught in the way of the good life; hopefully then, means might be found for our future amendment and spiritual growth.

[1]*Ecclesiastes 6:2* [2]*Luke 12:19* [3]*Luke 12:15, Proverbs 19:1*
[4]*Rom. 7:24, II Cor. 5:2* [5]*Psalm 25:17* [6]*Romans 8:22*
[7]*Colossians 3:2* [8]*II Corinthians 4:18* [9]*Rom.13:11, Heb.10:35*
[10]*Psalm 66:12* [11]*II Corinthians 5:4* [12]*Genesis 6:5, 8:21*
[13]*I Thessalonians 5:3*

Chapter 23

On the Thought of Death

The hour of our death will soon come; see then how it will be with you in another world; for today a man is, tomorrow he is not.[1]

And when he is out of sight, he is quickly out of mind.

How dull and hard is the man's heart who thinks only of the present and does not look for what is to come!

You should so order all your thoughts and actions as if you were to die today.

If you had a good conscience, you would not greatly fear death.[2]

It would be better to take heed not to sin than to be afraid of death.

If you are not prepared for death today, how will you be ready tomorrow?[3]

Tomorrow is uncertain, and you do not even know that you will have a tomorrow![4]

2. What good is it to live long if we are so little the better?

Alas! Long life does not always bring amendment, but often rather adds to our guilt.

O that we might spend even one day in this world thoroughly well!

Many count years since their conversion, and yet there is but little fruit of amendment.

If it is a fearful thing to die, it may be even more fearful to live long.

Happy are those who keep the hour of death always in mind and are daily prepared to die.

If you have ever seen a man die, remember that you also must pass the same way.

3. In the morning, consider that you may die before night, and when night comes, do not dare to boast yourself of the morrow.

Always be ready, and live in such a way that death will never find you unprepared.

Remember that many die suddenly and unexpectedly, for the Son of Man will come in an hour when we think not.[5]

When that last hour comes, you will begin to think very differently of your past life than you had before, and you will mourn bitterly that you have been so careless and remiss.

4. Happy and wise is he who strives to be such now in life as he desires to be found at death!

Perfect contempt of the world, fervent desire to make progress in virtue, love of discipline, the fruitful labor of repentance, ready obedience, the denial of self, and a willing endurance of all adversities for the love of Christ—

these things will give us great confidence that we shall die well.

While you are in good health you may do much good; but when you are sick, who knows what you can do?

Few are made better by sickness, and those who go on pilgrimage frequently are seldom made holy by it.

5. Do not trust in your friends and kinsfolk, and do not put off your soul's welfare to the future; for men will forget you sooner than you think.

It is better to look to it now, and send some good on ahead of you, than to trust to the help of others.

If you are not careful for yourself now, who will be careful for you hereafter?

Now the time is very precious. Now is the day of salvation; now is the accepted time.[6]

But alas for sorrow! that you should not spend your time more profitably, in which you could win everlasting life!

The time will come when you will desire one day, yea, one hour in which to change, but I do not know whether you will obtain it.

6. O dearly beloved, from what great danger might you deliver yourself, from what great fear might you free yourself, if you would live in holy fear and mindfulness of death!

Strive to live now, so that in the hour of death you may rejoice rather than fear.

Learn now to die to the world, so that you may begin then to live with Christ.[7]

Learn now to despise all earthly things, so that you may then freely go to Christ.[8]

Discipline your body now by works meet for repentance, so that you may then have a sure and steadfast hope of salvation.[9]

7. Ah, foolish one! Why do you expect to live long when you are not sure of a single day?[10]

How many have been deceived and suddenly have been snatched away from the body!

How often have you heard how one was slain by the sword, another was drowned, or another man fell and broke his neck; this man died eating, that man playing? One died by fire, one by pestilence, another at the hand of thieves. Thus death is the end of all and man's life as a shadow suddenly flees and is gone.[11]

8. Who will remember you when you are dead, and who will pray for you?

Do now, even now, beloved soul, all you can, for you do not know when you will die or what will happen to you after your death.

Now while you have time, lay up for yourself everlasting riches.[12]

Think on nothing but the salvation of your soul, and care for nothing but the things of God.

Make yourself friends now by honoring the saints of God and imitating their actions, so that when you fail here, they may receive you into eternal habitations.[13]

9. Keep yourself as a pilgrim and stranger on the earth who has nothing to do with the affairs of this world.[14]

Keep your heart free and lifted up to God, because we have here no abiding city.[15]

Send to Heaven daily your prayers, with sighs and tears, so that your spirit may be found worthy to pass happily after death to the Lord.

[1]*Job 9:25, 26* [2]*Luke 12:37* [3]*Matthew 24:44* [4]*James 4:14*
[5]*Matt. 24:44* [6]*II Cor. 6:2* [7]*Romans 6:1* [8]*Luke 14:33*
[9]*I Cor. 9:27* [10]*Luke 12:20* [11]*Job 14:2, James 4:4* [12]*Matt. 6:20, Lk. 12:33*
[13]*Luke 16:9* [14]*I Peter 2:11* [15]*Hebrews 13:14*

Chapter 24

On the Judgment and Punishment of Sins

In all things, look to the end, and how you will stand before a strict Judge, from whom nothing is hid, who is not bribed with gifts, who accepts no excuses; but will judge righteous judgment.

O most miserable and foolish sinner, who sometimes fears the countenance of an angry man, what will you answer to God, who knows all your misdeeds?

Why do you not provide for yourself against that day of judgment, when no man can be excused or defended by another, but every one shall have to bear his burden himself?

Now your labor is fruitful; now is your weeping acceptable, your sorrow well pleasing to God and cleansing to your soul.

2. Even here on earth the patient man finds a great and wholesome purification; when suffering injuries, he grieves more for the other's malice than for his own suffering; when he prays heartily for those who despitefully use him, and forges them from his heart; when he is not slow to ask pardon from others; when he is swifter moved to compassion than to anger; when he frequently does violence to himself and strives to bring his flesh wholly under subjection to the spirit. It is better now to purge out our sins and cut short our vices than to reserve them to be purged away in the future.

Verily we deceive ourselves through the inordinate love we bear to the flesh.

3. What other things shall that fire feed on but your sins?

The more you spare yourself and follow the flesh, the harder will be your calamity afterwards, and the more fuel are you heaping up for the flame.

For in whatever a man has sinned, in these shall he be more heavily punished.

There the slothful shall be pricked forward with burning goads, and the gluttons be tormented with intolerable hunger and thirst.

There the luxurious and the lovers of pleasure will be plunged into burning pitch and stinking brimstone, and the envious shall howl like mad dogs for very grief.

4. There is no vice which shall not be visited with its own proper punishment.

The proud shall be filled with utter confusion, and the covetous shall be pinched with miserable poverty.

One hour of pain there shall be more bitter than a century here spent in the gravest penance.

There shall be no quiet, no comfort for the damned there; but here there is now and then some respite from pain and the enjoyment of solace from friends.

Be solicitous and sorrowful for your sins now, so that in the day of judgment you may have security with the blessed.

For then shall the righteous stand in great boldness before the face of those who have afflicted them and kept them down.

Then he will stand to judge who now humbly submits himself to the judgments of men.

Then the poor and humble will have great confidence, and the proud will fear on every side.

5. Then shall it be seen that he was the wise man in this world, who learned to be a fool and despised for Christ.

Then shall every tribulation patiently borne delight us,

while the mouth of the ungodly will be stopped.

Then shall every godly man rejoice and every irreligious man mourn.

Then the afflicted flesh shall more rejoice than if it had always been nourished in delights.

Then the humble garment shall shine, and the precious robe shall hide itself as under a shade.

Then the little poor cottage shall be more praised than the gilded palace.

Then shall enduring patience have more might than all the power of the world.

Then simple obedience shall be more highly exalted than all worldly cleverness.

6. Then a pure and good conscience shall rejoice more than learned philosophy.

Then contempt of riches will have more weight than all the treasures of the children of this world.

Then you will find more consolation from your devout prayers than in having fared daintily.

Then you will be more glad for having kept silence than for having talked too much.

Then good works will be of greater value than many beautiful words.

Then a strict life and hard penance will be more pleasing than all the delights of this earth.

Learn now to suffer a little, so that you may then be able to escape far more grievous sufferings.

Try first here what you are to suffer hereafter.

If you can now endure so little, how will you be able to endure eternal torments?

If a little suffering now makes you so impatient, what will hellfire do hereafter?

Behold now you cannot have two joys: to delight yourself here in the world and then reign with Christ hereafter.

7. Suppose that up to this very day you had always lived in honor and worldly delights, what good would it all be to you if you were to die at this instant?

All then is vanity but to love God and to serve Him only.

He who loves God with all his heart is neither afraid of death, nor punishment, nor judgment, nor Hell; for perfect love gives sure access to God.

But he who still takes delight in sin, it is no wonder that he dreads both death and judgment.

Yet it is good, although your love of God is not yet strong enough to withhold you from sin, that at least the fear of Hell should restrain you.

But he who puts aside the fear of God cannot long continue in good; but shall quickly run into the snares of the devil.

Chapter 25

On the Zealous Amendment of Life

Be vigilant and diligent in the service of God, and consider often why you came here and why you have left the world. Was it not that you might live for God and become a spiritual man?

Be fervent then in your spiritual progress, for soon you will receive the reward of your labors. There will then be no more fear or sorrow for you.

You labor but a little now, and you will find great rest, even everlasting joy.

If you continue faithful and fervent in your work, without doubt God will be faithful and liberal with you in His rewards.

You must have a good hope of gaining the victory,[1] but

you must not think yourself secure, lest you then grow negligent or be puffed up.

2. A certain man, who often fluctuated anxiously between fear and hope, one day was oppressed with grief. Humbly he prostrated himself in a church before the altar in prayer. Within himself he said, "Oh, if only I knew that I should yet persevere to the end of my life!" All at once he heard within himself the divine answer, saying, "What would you do if you knew you would persevere? Do now what you would then, and you will be well secure."

Being comforted and strengthened by this, he committed himself to the will of God, and his anxious wavering ceased.

He had no desire to search curiously any further to know what should happen to him. Instead, he labored to understand what was the perfect and acceptable will of God for the beginning and accomplishing of every good work.[2]

3. "Trust in the Lord and do good," says the psalmist, "so you will dwell in the land and enjoy security."[3]

One thing deters many in their spiritual progress and fervent amendment of life: that is the dread of the difficulty or the cost of the conflict.

But in truth those who make the greatest effort to overcome those things that are most troublesome and repugnant to them advance most beyond others in virtue.

A man profits most and merits greater grace where he most overcomes himself and mortifies himself in spirit.

4. All men do not have the same things to overcome and put to death.

But he who is diligent and zealous will be able to make greater progress than another who is of a more temperate natural disposition but less fervent in his pursuit of virtue.

Two things help a man much to the amendment of life: a violent withdrawal from those very things to which his nature is viciously inclined; and earnest labor for that good which is most lacking.

Strive also very earnestly to avoid in yourself and to overcome those faults which most frequently offend you in others.

5. Seek some spiritual profit wherever you are, and if you see or hear of any good examples, stir up yourself to imitate them.

If you observe anything in others worthy of reproof, be careful not to do the same, and if at any time you have done it, strive quickly to amend yourself.

As you observe others, so also are you observed by others.

How good and pleasant a thing it is to see brethren fervent and devout, well mannered and well disciplined!

How sad and grievous it is to see them living in a disorderly way, not practicing that for which they are called!

How hurtful a thing it is when they neglect the good purposes of their calling, and busy themselves with things which have not been committed to them!

6. Be mindful of the profession you have made and always keep before the eyes of your mind your crucified Savior.

You have good reason to be ashamed when you look at the life of Jesus Christ, that you have not yet tried to conform to Him more, even though you have long been in the way of God.

He who will inwardly and devoutly exercise himself in the most blessed life and passion of our Lord will find everything there that is necessary for him, so that he will have no need to seek anything beyond Jesus.

Oh, if Jesus crucified did but come into our hearts, how

quickly and completely we would be taught everything necessary for us!

7. A fervent Religious takes and bears well all that is commanded him.

But a negligent and lukewarm Religious has trouble upon trouble and is afflicted on all sides, because he is without inward consolation and cannot seek outward comforts.

A Religious who does not live according to his discipline opens himself to much mischief, even to the ruin of his soul.

He who seeks freedom and ease will always be in anguish and sorrow, for one thing or another will always displease him.

8. Observe how Religious in other communities or orders live who are under a strict monastic life.

They seldom go forth from their seclusion; they eat the poorest fare, their clothing is coarse. They work much, they speak little, they have long prayer watches; they rise very early and spend much time in prayer. They read often, and discipline themselves carefully.

Consider the Carthusians, the Cistercians, and the monks and nuns of various orders, how they rise every night to sing praises to the Lord.

Therefore it would be a shame to you if you were slothful in so holy a work, when so many are beginning to laud and praise our Lord.

9. Oh, that we had nothing else to do but always to praise the Lord with our mouth and our whole heart.

Truly if we never needed to eat or drink or sleep, but always might praise Him and be mindful only of spiritual things, we would be much more happy than we are now, when we are bound to serve the needs of the body.

Would there were no such needs, but only the spiritual

refreshments of the soul, which, alas for sorrow! we taste too seldom.

10. When a man comes to such maturity that he seeks no consolation in any created thing, then he begins perfectly to relish God. Then he will be contented with everything that comes, whatever may befall him.

He will then neither rejoice in having much nor be sorrowful in having little. He will entirely and confidently commit himself to God, who is to him all in all, to whom nothing perishes or dies, to whom all things live and at whose command they instantly serve.

11. Remember always your destination and that time lost never returns. Without care and diligence you will never acquire virtue.

If you begin to grow lukewarm, it will begin to go evil with you.

But if you give yourself to zeal, you will find great peace and your labors will grow lighter by the help of God's grace and your own love of virtue.

It is harder work to resist vices and passions than to toil at bodily labors.

He who does not avoid small faults will little by little fall into greater ones.

You will always rejoice in the evening if you have spent the day well.

Be watchful over yourself, stir up yourself, admonish yourself, and regardless of what becomes of others, do not neglect yourself.

The more violence you use against your self life, the greater will be your spiritual progress. Amen.

[1]Literally *ad palmum pervenies:* to attain the palm. [2]*Rom. 12:2* [3]*Ps. 37:3*

The Second Book

Admonitions Concerning
The Inner Life

Chapter 1

On the Inner Life

"The kingdom of God is within you," says the Lord.[1] Turn, therefore, with your whole heart to the Lord, forsake this wretched world, and your soul will find rest.

Learn to despise outward things and to give yourself to those that are within, and you will see the kingdom of God come within yourself.

"For the kingdom of God is peace and joy in the Holy Spirit";[2] and it is not given to the wicked.

Christ will come to you and will show you His own consolations if you prepare Him a worthy dwelling place in your heart.

All His glory and beauty is within,[3] and there He delights to dwell.

He often visits the inner man, and has sweet discourse with him, giving him pleasant solace, much peace, and an intimate closeness, exceeding wonderful.

2. O faithful soul, come then and prepare your heart for this Bridegroom, that He may vouchsafe to come and dwell within you.

For He says Himself: "If any man love Me, he will keep My words, and We will come to him and make Our abode with him."[4]

Give place, then, for Christ and deny entrance to all others.

When you have Christ, you are rich and He alone is sufficient for you. He will be your provider and your faithful helper in every necessity, so you will not need to trust in men.

Men soon change and quickly fail, but Christ abides forever and stands by us firmly to the end.[5]

3. There is no great confidence to be put in frail and mortal man, however helpful and dear to us: nor should we be too grieved if he sometimes turns and opposes us.

They who are on your side today may turn against you tomorrow, and often they turn like the wind.

Put your whole trust in God,[6] and let Him be your love and fear above everything. He will answer for you Himself and will do for you what is best.

Here we have no abiding city.[7] Wherever you may be, you are a stranger and pilgrim, and never will you find perfect rest until you are fully united to Christ.

4. Why do you look around you here, since this is not the place of your rest? Your rest must be in heavenly things, and you must look on all earthly things as transitory and passing away.

All things pass away, and you together with them.

Beware that you do not cleave to them, lest you be caught up with the love of them and so perish. Let your thoughts be on the Most High, and your prayers directed to Christ without ceasing.

If you cannot always contemplate high and heavenly things, rest yourself in the passion of Christ, and willingly dwell in His blessed wounds.

If you flee devoutly to the wounds and precious marks of Jesus, you will feel great comfort in every trouble: neither will you care greatly for the slights of men, and you will grieve little for whatever evil words are spoken against you.

5. Christ was despised by all men in the world, and in His greatest need was forsaken by His acquaintances and friends, and left in the midst of reproaches.[8]

He was willing to suffer wrongs and to be despised, and do you dare complain of anything?

Christ had many adversaries and backbiters; do you wish to have all men as your friends and benefactors?

How shall your patience win its crown, if no adversity befall you?[9]

If you are not willing to suffer opposition, how will you be a friend of Christ?

Bear up with Christ and for Christ, if you desire to reign with Christ.

6. If but once you had entered completely into the heart of Jesus, and had but tasted a little of His ardent love, then you would not be concerned about your convenience or inconvenience, but rather would rejoice in reproaches if they come upon you, because the love of Jesus makes a man despise himself.

A lover of Jesus and of truth, a truly inward Christian and one who is free from inordinate affections, can freely turn himself to God and rise in spirit above his self-concerns, and fruitfully rest.

7. He who esteems things as they are in reality, and not as they are said or thought to be, is truly wise, taught of God rather than man.

He who knows how to live inwardly, to set small value on outward things, neither requires special places nor awaits proper times for performing devout exercises.

A man of the inward life quickly recollects himself, because he never gives himself entirely to outward things.

He is not hindered by outward labor or business, which may be necessary for the time, but as things happen, he adjusts himself to them.

He who is well ordered and disposed within himself is not interested in the strange and perverse behavior of others.

A man is hindered and distracted in proportion as he draws outward things to himself.

8. If your spirit were right and you were thoroughly purified from sin, all things would work out for your good and profit.[10]

The reason that many things displease and trouble you is that you are not yet completely dead to self, nor separated from all earthly things.

Nothing so defiles and entangles the heart of man as the impure love of things created.

If you reject outward comfort, you will be able to contemplate heavenly things and frequently to be inwardly filled with joy.

[1]*Luke 17:21* [2]*Rom. 14:17* [3]*Ps. 14:13* [4]*John 14:23*
[5]*John 12:34* [6]*I Pet. 5:7* [7]*Heb. 13:14* [8]*Matt. 12:24, 16:21, John 20:20*
[9]*II Tim. 2:5* [10]*Rom. 8:28*

Chapter 2

On Humble Submission Before Reproof

Do not concern yourself much with who is for you and who against you, but give all your thought and care to this, that God is with you in everything you do.

Have a good conscience, and God will defend you well.

He whom God helps will never be hurt by the malice of man.

If you can be silent and suffer, you will surely see the help of the Lord come in your need.

He knows the time and the way to deliver you, so you ought to resign yourself to Him.

God is able to help and to deliver from all confusion.

It nevertheless often helps to keep us in greater humility that others know and rebuke our faults.

2. When a man humbles himself for his faults, then he easily pacifies others and quickly satisfies those who were angry with him.

God protects and delivers the humble.[1] The humble He loves and comforts. To the humble man He inclines Himself; to the humble He gives abundant grace; and after he has been cast down, He raises him to glory.

He reveals His secrets to the humble and tenderly draws and invites him to Himself.

Though he suffer confusion and reproof, the humble man yet has good peace, because he trusts in God and not in the world.

Never think you have made any spiritual progress until you esteem yourself inferior to all.

[1] *James 3, Job 5:11*

Chapter 3

On the Peaceable Man

First keep yourself in peace, and then you will be able to make peace among others.

A peaceable man does more good than one who is very learned.

A passionate man turns even good to evil and easily believes the worst.

A good and peaceable man turns all things to good.

He who is in peace is not suspicious of anyone, but he

who is discontented and troubled is tossed about with various suspicions. He is neither quiet himself, nor does he allow others to be quiet.

He often speaks what he should not, and omits that which he should have done.

He takes great notice of what others should do, and neglects that which he himself should do.[1]

So, first be zealous against yourself, and then you may justly show zeal for your neighbor's good.[2]

2. You know very well how to excuse and explain your own deeds, but you are not willing to accept the excuses of others.

It would be better to accuse yourself and excuse your brother.

If you want to have others bear with you, you should also bear with others.[3]

See how far you are still from true charity and humility; such as these are not able to be angry with anyone but themselves.

It is no great thing to associate with the good and gentle, for this is naturally pleasing to all, and everyone welcomes peace and loves best those who agree with him.

But to be able to live peaceably with difficult and perverse persons who lack good manners, who are willfully ignorant and undisciplined, or with those who constantly disagree with us–this is a great grace and a most commendable and manly feat.

3. There are some who keep themselves in peace and live at peace with others.

But there are some who are not at peace in themselves and will not allow others to be in peace. They are troublesome to others, but always more troublesome to themselves.

And there are others who keep themselves in peace and seek to bring others back into peace.

Nevertheless, all our peace in this miserable life lies in humble endurance rather than in not feeling what is against us.

He who knows best how to suffer will enjoy the most peace. That man is a conqueror of himself, lord of the world, a friend of Christ, and an heir of Heaven.

[1]*Matthew 7:3* [2]*Acts 22:3* [3]*Gal. 6:2, I Cor. 13:7*

Chapter 4

On Purity and Simplicity

By two wings a man is lifted above earthly things–simplicity and purity.

Simplicity should mark our purpose; purity our affections. Simplicity looks toward God and purity takes hold of Him and tastes Him.[1]

If you are free from all inordinate love, no good action will be distasteful to you.

If you intend and seek nothing but the will of God and the good of your neighbor, you will enjoy inner freedom thoroughly.

If your heart were right, then every created thing would be as a living mirror to you and a holy book of doctrine.

There is nothing created so small and contemptible that it does not show the goodness of God.[2]

2. If you were good and pure inwardly in your soul, you would be able to see and understand all things without impediment and understand them aright.

A pure heart penetrates both Heaven and Hell.

As a man is inwardly in his heart, so he judges outwardly.

If there is any true joy in the world, surely a man of a pure heart possesses it.

And if there is any tribulation and anguish, an evil conscience knows it best.

As iron put in the fire loses its rust and becomes all red and glowing, so he who turns himself wholly to God puts off sluggishness and is transformed into a new man.

3. When a man begins to grow lukewarm, then he fears a little labor, and gladly receives outward comforts of the world and the flesh.

But when he begins to overcome himself perfectly and to walk manfully in the way of God, then he lightly regards those things which before seemed so burdensome to him.

[1]*Psalm 34:8* [2]*Romans 1:20*

Chapter 5

On Knowing Ourselves

We cannot trust much to ourselves, because we often lack grace and self-understanding.

There is but little light in us, and even that which we have we quickly lose by negligence.

Many times we do not perceive how blind we are within.

We often do evil, and in defending it do even worse.

Sometimes we are moved with passion and think that it is zeal.

We reprove small faults in others, and pass over our own greater faults.

We are quick enough to feel and weigh what we suffer from others, but we think little of what others suffer from us.

He who would well and rightly weigh his own actions would not be disposed to judge others harshly.

2. The man who is truly turned to God inwardly takes heed of himself before all else, and he who diligently attends to his own soul easily keeps silence in regard to others.

You will never be a spiritually minded and godly man unless you pass over with silence the affairs of others, and look especially to yourself.

If you attend wholly to God and yourself, what you see around you will affect you but little.

Where are you when you are not with yourself? And when you have looked at everything and have considered at length the deeds of others, what profit is it to you if you have neglected yourself?

If you would have peace in your soul and true unity, you must put all other things aside, and attend to yourself.

3. You will make great progress if you will keep yourself free from all worldly cares.

You will lose greatly if you set great value upon any temporal thing.

Let nothing be great to you, nothing high, nothing pleasing, nothing acceptable, but God Himself or that which is of God.

Consider all creature comforts but vain.

A soul that loves God despises all things other than God.

God alone is eternal and of infinite greatness, filling all creation. He is the solace of the soul and the true joy of the heart.

Chapter 6

On the Joy of a Good Conscience

The glory of a good man is the testimony of a good conscience.[1] Have a good conscience and you will always have joy. A good conscience can bear very much and is very cheerful in the midst of adversity.

A bad conscience is always fearful and uneasy.[2]

You will rest peacefully if your heart does not condemn you.

Never rejoice unless you have done well.

Wicked men never know true joy nor feel inward peace, because "There is no peace to the wicked," says the Lord.[3]

And if they should say, "We are in peace, no evil will befall us,[4] and who will dare hurt us?" do not believe them; for all of a sudden the wrath of God will arise, their deeds will come to nothing, and their thoughts will perish.[5]

2. To glory in tribulation is not a hard thing for one who truly loves God; for so to glory is to glory in the Cross of our Lord Jesus Christ.

The glory given and received by men is fleeting and shortlived.

The glory of this world is always accompanied by sorrow.

The glory of the good is in their consciences, not in the tongues of men. The gladness of the righteous is in God and from God, and their joy is in the truth.

He who desires true and everlasting glory does not value the glory of the world.

And he who seeks temporal glory, or who does not despise it from his soul, shows that he has but little love for the glory of Heaven.

He enjoys great tranquility of heart who cares neither for the praise nor the vituperations of men.

3. He will easily be at peace and content whose conscience is clean.

You are no more holy if you are praised, nor worse if you are reproached.

What you are, you are, and words cannot make you greater than you are in the eyes of God.

If you consider well what you are within yourself, you will not care what men say about you outwardly.

Man looks on the appearance, but God looks on the heart.[6] Man considers the deeds, but God weighs the motives.

To be always doing well and to think that you have done but little is the sign of the humble soul.

To be unwilling to have any created being for our comfort is a sign of great purity and inward trust.

4. He who seeks no testimony on his behalf from the outside, shows that he has wholly committed himself to God.

"For it is not the man who commends himself that is accepted," says St. Paul, "but the man whom the Lord commends."[7]

To walk inwardly with God, and not to be held by any outward affections is the state of a spiritual man.

[1] *I Corinthians 1:31* [2] *Wisdom 17:11* [3] *Isaiah 57:21*
[4] *Luke 12:19* [5] *Psalms 73:18, 19* [6] *I Samuel 16:7*
[7] *II Corinthians 10:18*

Chapter 7

On Loving Jesus Above All Things

Blessed is he who knows how good it is to love Jesus, and to despise himself for the sake of Jesus.

He must give up every other love for this Beloved, for Jesus would be loved alone above all things.

The love of created things is deceitful and unstable, but the love of Jesus is faithful and abiding.

He who cleaves to created things will fall with them. He who embraces Jesus will stand firm in Him forever.

Love Him, and hold Him as your friend, for He will not forsake you when all others leave you, nor allow you finally to perish.

One day you must be separated from all, whether you will it or not.

2. Therefore, living or dying, keep close to Jesus and commit yourself to His faithfulness, who alone can help you when all else fails you.

Your Beloved is of such a nature that He will admit of no rival, but would have your heart's love for Himself only, and would reign there on His own throne.

If you would learn to empty yourself of all created things, Jesus would readily dwell with you.

Whatever trust you put in men, apart from Jesus, will be little better than lost.

Do not trust or lean on a reed shaken by the wind, for all flesh is grass and all its glory shall fade and wither as the flower of the field.[1]

3. If you look only on the outward appearance of men, you will soon be deceived.

For if you seek comfort and gain in others, you will feel thereby great spiritual loss.

If you seek Jesus in all things, you will surely find Jesus.

If you seek yourself, you will find yourself indeed, but to your own great loss.

For truly a man is more hurtful to himself, if he seek not Jesus, than all the world and all his enemies.

[1]*Isaiah 40:6*

CHAPTER 8

On the Intimate Friendship of Jesus

When Jesus is present, all is well and nothing seems difficult; but when Jesus is absent, everything is hard.

When Jesus does not speak inwardly to us, all other comfort is nothing worth; but if Jesus speak but one word, great consolation abounds.

Did not Mary arise immediately from her weeping when Martha said to her, "The Master is here and is calling for you"?[1]

Happy hour! When Jesus calls us from tears to joy of spirit.

How parched and hard-hearted you are without Jesus! How foolish and vain if you desire anything beyond Jesus!

Is not this a greater loss to you than if you were to lose the whole world? [2]

2. What can the world confer on you without Jesus?

To be without Jesus is the gravest Hell; and to be with Jesus is a sweet paradise.

If Jesus is with you, no enemy can grieve or hurt you.[3]

Whoever finds Jesus finds a good treasure, yes, a good above all good.[4]

And he who loses Jesus loses very much, yes, more than all the world.

He is most poor who lives without Jesus; and he is most rich who is dear to Jesus.[5]

3. It is a great art to know how to live with Jesus, and to know how to hold Jesus is great wisdom.

Be humble and peaceable, and Jesus will be with you.[6]

Be devout and quiet, and Jesus will abide with you.

You may quickly drive Jesus away and lose His favor if you turn back to outward things.

And if you drive Him from you and lose Him, to whom will you turn, and what friend will you then seek?

Without a friend you cannot live well, and if Jesus is not your friend above all, you will be exceedingly sad and desolate.

Therefore you act very foolishly if you put your trust or begin to rejoice in any other.[7]

It is better to have all the world against us than that Jesus be offended with us.

Of all therefore that are dear and beloved to you, let Jesus alone be most beloved.

4. Let all be loved for Jesus' sake, but Jesus for His own sake.

Jesus Christ alone is to be loved exclusively, because He alone is proved good and faithful before all other friends.

In Him and for Him let friends and foes be dear to you. All these are to be prayed for, that all may know and love Him.[8]

Never desire to be the object of praise or love above others, for that belongs only to God, who has none like Himself.

Neither desire that anyone's heart be set on you, and do

not set your heart on the love of anyone, but let Jesus be in you and in every good man and woman.

5. Be pure and free inwardly, and do not become entangled by any created thing.

You should be naked and open before God, ever carrying a pure heart towards Him, if you would know rest and feel how sweet the Lord is.

And truly, unless you are preceded and drawn by His grace, you will never attain to that happiness of forsaking and leaving all in order that you may be inwardly knit and united to Him.

For when the grace of God comes to a man, then he is enabled to do all things, and when it departs, he is weak and poor, and as it were, given up to afflictions.

In this case, you should not be downcast or despairing, but should resign yourself calmly to the will of God, to bear whatever comes upon you for the glory of Jesus Christ; for summer follows winter, after the night, day returns, and after the storm, a great calm.

[1]*John 11:28* [2]*Matthew 16:26* [3]*Romans 8:35*
[4]*Matthew 13:44* [5]*Luke 12:21* [6]*Proverbs 3:17*
[7]*Galatians 6:14* [8]*Matt. 5:44, Luke 6:27, 28*

Chapter 9

On the Lack of Comfort

It is not hard to despise human comfort when we have that which is divine.

It is a great thing indeed to be able to bear the loss of both human and divine comfort, and for God's honor to be willing to endure this desolation of heart, to seek oneself in nothing, and not to look to one's own merit.

What great thing is it to be cheerful and devout when grace comes to you? That is an hour desired by everyone.

It is pleasant to ride when carried by the grace of God.

And what wonder is it if he does not feel his burden when he is borne up by the Almighty and led by the Sovereign Guide?

2. We gladly hold on to anything for solace and comfort and it is difficult to cast off the false love of self.

The blessed martyr St. Lawrence, through the love of God, mightily overcame the love of the world and of himself, despising what seemed delightsome in the world. For the love of Christ he patiently suffered when Pope Sixtus, whom he dearly loved, was taken from him.[1]

He therefore overcame the love of man by the love of the Creator, choosing rather what pleased God than human comfort.

So also, you must learn to give up even a near and dear friend for the love of God.

And do not think it hard when you are forsaken by a friend, since you know that we must all at the last be separated from one another.

3. A man must strive long and mightily with himself before he can learn fully to master himself and turn his whole affection towards God.

When a man puts trust in himself, he easily comes to depend on human comforts.

But one who truly loves Christ and is a diligent seeker of virtue does not lean on these comforts nor seek such sensible sweetness, but chooses rather hard trials and heavy labors for Christ.

4. When God therefore gives you spiritual comfort, receive it with thankfulness; but know that it is a gift of God, not your deserving.

Do not be proud, nor take too much joy in it, nor be vainly presumptuous. Rather be more humble on account of the gift, more careful and cautious in your actions; for the hour of comfort will pass away and temptation will follow.

When consolation is removed from you, do not immediately despair, but wait in humility and patience for the heavenly visitation; for God is able to give back again more ample consolation.

This is nothing new or strange to those who have experience in the ways of God; for the great saints and ancient prophets often experienced such changes.

5. One said at the time when grace was with him, "I said in my prosperity, 'I shall never be moved.' "[2]

But afterward, when grace was withdrawn, he said, "Thou didst turn Thy face from me, and I was troubled."

Yet in the meantime he did not despair, but sought the Lord more earnestly, saying, "Unto Thee, O Lord, will I cry, and I will pray to my God."

At length he received the fruit of his prayer and testifies that he was heard, saying, "The Lord hath heard me and hath had mercy on me; the Lord hath become my helper."

But how? "Thou hast turned my sorrow into joy," he says, "and Thou hast compassed me about with gladness."

If great saints were so dealt with, we that are weak and poor should not despair if we sometimes wax hot or cold; for the Spirit comes and goes according to the good pleasure of His own will.[3] It was for this cause that blessed Job says, "Thou dost visit him every morning and test him suddenly."[4]

6. On what then can I hope, or in what can I trust, but only in the great mercy of God and only in hope of heavenly grace?

For whether I have with me good men, devout brethren, or faithful friends, whether holy books, fine treatises or sweet hymns and songs, all these help but little and are of little comfort when bereft of grace and left in my own poverty.

At such time there is no better remedy than patience and the denial of myself according to the will of God.[5]

7. I have never found anyone so spiritual and devout as not to have at times a withdrawal of grace or to feel some decrease of fervor.

There was never a saint so highly rapt or illuminated, who early or late was not tempted.

For he is not worthy of the high gift of the contemplation of God who has not been exercised by some tribulation for God's sake.

For temptation going before is often the sign of consolation to follow.

To those who have been proved by temptations, heavenly comfort is promised. Therefore He says, "To him that overcomes will I give to eat of the tree of life."[6]

8. Divine consolation is given to a man so that he may be stronger when adversities come.

But temptation follows so that he may not be puffed up in pride by such benefit.

The devil does not sleep, neither is the flesh as yet dead: therefore you must prepare yourself for battle, for you have enemies on the right side and on the left, who never rest.

[1]Pope Sixtus II was martyred in Rome in 258 A.D. Six deacons were put to death with him. St. Lawrence, the seventh deacon, was killed four days later. These two men are among the most honored martyrs of Rome in the early centuries.

[2]*Cf. Psalm 30:6-11* [3]*John 3:8* [4]*Job 7:18*
[5]*Luke 9:23* [6]*Revelation 2:7*

Chapter 10

On Gratitude for the Grace of God

Why do you seek rest, since you were born to labor? Prepare yourself for patience rather than consolations, to bear the Cross rather than to rejoice.

What worldly man is there who would not gladly receive spiritual comfort and joy if he could always have it?

For spiritual comforts exceed all the delights of the world and the pleasures of the flesh.

For all worldly delights are either vain or unclean, while spiritual delights alone are pleasant and honest, springing from virtues and poured forth by God into pure minds.

But such divine consolations no man can have as he would, for the time of temptation is never far away.

2. A false liberty of mind and a great confidence in self are very opposite to heavenly visitations.

God does well in giving the grace of consolation, but man does evil in not returning it all again to Him with thanksgiving.

Therefore the gifts of grace cannot flow in us, because we are ungrateful to the Giver, and do not return them wholly to the Fountain from whom all good comes.[1]

Grace is always given to those who are ready to yield

thanks for grace received, but from the proud is taken what is freely given to the humble.

3. I do not desire any consolation that takes away any sting of conscience, nor any contemplation that leads to pride.

For all that is high is not holy; nor is all that is sweet good, nor every desire pure; nor is everything that is dear to us pleasing to God.

I willingly accept that grace whereby I may be made humbler, more careful, and more ready to renounce myself.

He who is taught by the gift of grace and schooled by its withdrawals, will not dare to think that any goodness comes from himself, but will openly confess that he is poor and naked.

Render to God what is God's[2] and ascribe to yourself what is yours: that is, give thanks to God for His grace, and acknowledge that to yourself alone belong your fault and the fitting punishment of the fault.

4. Always put yourself in the lowest place and the highest will be given you; for the highest cannot stand without the lowest.

The greatest saints before God are least in their own judgments, and the more glorious they are, the more humble within themselves are they.

Those who are full of truth and the glory of heaven are not desirous of vain glory.

Those who are firmly settled and grounded in God can in no way be proud.

They who ascribe to God whatever good they have received do not seek glory of one another, but that glory which is from God alone. Desiring above all things that God may be praised in themselves and in all His saints, they constantly press on for this very thing.

Be thankful for even the least and you will be worthy to receive greater things.

Let the least be to you as greatest, and the most contemptible as a special gift.

If you consider the dignity of the Giver, no gift will seem little or too mean to value. For that cannot be small which is given by the Most High God.

Yes, even though He give punishment and stripes, it ought to be acceptable because whatever He permits to happen to us is always for our salvation.

Let him who desires to retain the favor of God be thankful for grace given and patient when it is taken away. Let him pray that it may return; let him be careful and humble in spirit, that he does not lose it.

[1]*James 1:17* [2]*Matthew 22:21*

Chapter 11

On the Fewness of the Lovers of the Cross of Jesus

Jesus has many lovers of His heavenly kingdom, but few bearers of His Cross.

He has many seekers of consolation, but few of tribulation.

He finds many companions at His feasting, but few at His fasting.

All desire to rejoice with Him; few are willing to endure anything for Him.

Many follow Jesus as far as the breaking of bread, but few

to the drinking of the cup of His Passion.[1]

Many reverence His miracles, but few will follow the shame of His Cross.

Many love Jesus as long as no adversities befall them.

Many praise and bless Him so long as they receive some consolation from Him.

But if Jesus hide Himself and leave them but for a brief time, they begin to complain or become overly despondent in mind.

2. They who love Jesus for Jesus' sake, and not for any comforts they receive, bless Him as readily in temptation and anguish of heart as in the state of highest consolation.

And though He never send them consolation, yet they would ever praise Him and give Him thanks.

3. O what power there is in the pure love of Jesus when it is not mixed with self-interest and self-love!

Are not those to be called hirelings who are always looking for consolations?

Do they not show by their actions that they are lovers of self rather than of Christ, who are always thinking of their own advantage and profit?[2]

Where can even one be found who is willing to serve God for nothing?

4. Rarely is there anyone who is so spiritual as to be thoroughly free from leaning on created things. His worth is beyond calculation!

If a man should give all he owns, yet it is nothing. And if he practice great penance, still it is little. And though he understand all knowledge, he is still far off.

And if he should have great virtue and be fervent in devotion, even yet there is much lacking, especially the one thing most necessary for him.

What is that? That forsaking all, he forsake himself, go wholly from himself, and keep nothing of self-love.[3]

And having done all things which he knows to be his duty, let him think that he has done nothing.

5. Let him not think that to be great which others esteem great, but let him in truth confess himself to be an unprofitable servant, as the Truth Himself says, "When you have done all things commanded you, say we are unprofitable servants."[4]

Then he may well be called poor in spirit, and he may well say with the prophet, "I am desolate and afflicted."[5]

Yet there is none richer, none freer, none more powerful than he, for he knows how to forsake himself and all, and truly put himself in the lowest place.

[1]*Luke 9:14, 22:41, 42* [2]*Philippians 2:21* [3]*Matthew 26:24*
[4]*Luke 17:10* [5]*Psalm 25:16*

Chapter 12

On the Royal Way of the Holy Cross

This seems to many to be a hard saying: "If any man will come after Me, let him deny himself, and take up his cross, and follow Me."[1]

But it will be much harder to hear these words at the last day: "Depart from me, ye cursed, into everlasting fire."[2]

For those who now gladly and willingly hear and follow the word of the Cross will not then fear lest they hear the sentence of everlasting damnation.

This sign of the Cross will appear in Heaven when the Lord comes to judgment.

Then all the servants of the Cross, who in their lifetime conformed themselves to the Crucified, shall draw near to Christ the Judge with great boldness.

2. Why do you dread to take up the Cross, since it is the very way to the kingdom of Heaven?

In the Cross is salvation; in the Cross is life; in the Cross is defense against our enemies; in the Cross is infusion of heavenly sweetness; in the Cross is strength of mind; in the Cross is joy of spirit; in the Cross is the height of virtue; in the Cross is the perfection of holiness.

There is no health of the soul nor hope of eternal life, but in the Cross.

Take up your Cross, therefore, and follow Jesus, and you will go into life eternal. He went before you bearing His own Cross[3] and died for you upon the Cross, that you might also bear your Cross and that you should be ready to die on the Cross.

For if you die with Him, you will also live with Him. And if you are partaker of His suffering, you will be also of His glory.[4]

3. Behold then, how on the Cross everything hangs, and how in dying on it everything depends. There is no other way to life and true inward peace, but the way of the holy Cross and of daily self-denial.

Go where you will, seek whatever you will, you will not find a higher way above nor a safer way below, than the way of the holy Cross.

Dispose everything according to your will and judgment, yet you will still find that you will have of necessity something to suffer, willingly or unwillingly, and so, you will always find the Cross.

For either you will feel pain in your body or in soul or suffer trouble of spirit.

4. You will feel sometimes forsaken by God, at other times you will be troubled by your neighbors, and what is more, you will sometimes be a burden to yourself.

Yet you cannot find remedy or comfort for your trouble as long as God wills you to bear it.

For God would have you learn to suffer tribulation without consolation, that you submit yourself wholly to Him and to become more humble by tribulation.

No man feels the suffering of Jesus so intensely as one who has suffered like things.

The Cross is always ready, therefore, and waits for you everywhere.

You cannot escape it wherever you run; for wherever you may go, you take yourself with you, and you will always find yourself.

Turn upward, turn downward, turn outward, turn inward, you will find the Cross everywhere, so you always need patience if you would have inward peace and win a lasting crown.

5. If you bear the Cross cheerfully, it will bear you and bring you to your desired goal, where there will be an end of suffering, though this cannot be here.

If you bear the Cross unwillingly, you make a great burden for yourself and greatly increase your load, though you will still have to bear it.

If you cast away one Cross, you will undoubtedly find another, and that perhaps a heavier one.

6. Do you think you can escape what no other mortal has been able to avoid? Which of the saints was without the Cross and trials in this world?

For not even our Lord Jesus Christ was ever one hour without some sorrow and pain as long as He lived here. "Christ," He says, "must needs suffer and rise again from the dead and so enter into His glory."[5] And how is it then that you seek another way than this royal way, which is the way of the holy Cross?

7. The whole life of Christ was Cross and martyrdom, and do you seek pleasure and joy for yourself?

You are wrong, you are wrong if you seek anything other than to suffer trials; for this whole mortal life is full of miseries and is marked on every side with crosses.

The further a man advances in spirit, so much heavier are the crosses he often finds, because the pain of his exile increases with his love.

8. Nevertheless this man, in so many ways afflicted, is not without some comfort, for he sees well that great fruit and benefit will be his by the bearing of his own Cross.

For while he willingly submits himself to such trial, then all the burden of tribulation is turned into assurance of divine consolation.

And the more the flesh is subdued by affliction, the more the spirit is strengthened by inward grace.

And sometimes it feels such comfort in adversities, that for desire to be conformed to the Cross of Christ, it would not be without sorrow and affliction;[6] for it believes that the more it bears for Him here, the more acceptable it will be to God.

It is not the virtue of man, but the grace of God that enables a frail man to attempt and love that which by nature he abhors and fears.

9. It is not man's way to bear the Cross, to love the Cross, to chasten the body and bring it into subjection to the spirit, to flee honors, to suffer being insulted, to despise self and to want to be despised, to endure all adversities and losses, and to desire no prosperity in this world.

If you trust in yourself, you will never be able to bring this about.

But if you trust in the Lord, strength will be given you from Heaven, and the world and the flesh will be made subject to your command.

If you are armed with faith and signed with the Cross of Christ, you will not fear your enemy the devil.

10. Set yourself, then, like a good and faithful servant of Christ to bear manfully the Cross of your Lord, who out of love for you was crucified.

Prepare yourself to bear many adversities and various kinds of troubles in this miserable life; for so it will be with you wherever you may be, or wherever you may hide yourself.

It must be so, and there is no remedy or way of escape from the tribulation of evils and sorrows, but to bear them patiently.

Drink lovingly of the cup of the Lord if you desire to be His friend and to have a part with Him.[7]

As for consolations, leave them to God to do as shall best please Him.

But prepare yourself to bear tribulations and account them the greatest comforts; for "the sufferings of this present time are not worthy to be compared with the glory that is to come"[8] even if you alone could suffer them all.

11. When you come to this, that tribulations are sweet and pleasant to you for Christ's sake, then you account that it is well with you, for you have found paradise on earth.

As long as suffering is grievous to you and you long to escape, so long will it be ill with you, and tribulations will follow you everywhere.

12. If you set yourself to that condition in which you should be, that is to suffer gladly for God and to die fully

to the world, then it will quickly be better with you and you will find peace.

Even if you, like St. Paul, were "caught up into the third heaven," you would not then be free from all adversity. For Jesus says, "I will show him how much he must suffer for the sake of my name."[9]

Suffering, therefore, awaits you if you would love Jesus and constantly serve Him.

13. Would to God you were worthy to suffer something for the name of Jesus![10] How great a glory would await you! What gladness among all the saints of God! How edified would be those around you!

For all men praise patience, but few are willing to suffer.

How right it is to be willing to suffer some little thing for Christ's sake, since many suffer much more grievous things for the world.

14. Know this for certain, you must lead a dying life. The more you die to yourself, the more you begin to live to God.

No man is fit to receive the understanding of heavenly things if he has not submitted himself to bear adversities for Christ.

Nothing is more acceptable to God, nothing more profitable to you in this world than to suffer cheerfully for Christ.

And if you had to choose, you should rather choose adversity for Christ than to be refreshed by a multitude of consolations, because you would thus be more like Christ and His saints.

For our merit and our spiritual advancement does not consist in comforts and sweetness, but in bearing great adversities and tribulations.

15. For surely if there had been anything better and more useful than suffering for the health of man's soul, Christ would certainly have shown it by word and example.

But He openly exhorts the disciples who follow Him and all others who desire to follow Him to bear the Cross, saying, "If any man would come after Me, let him deny himself and take up his cross and follow Me."[11]

So, all things searched and read, this is the final conclusion, that through much tribulation we must enter the kingdom of God.[12]

[1]*Matthew 16:24* [2]*Matthew 25:41* [3]*Luke 14:27*
[4]*II Tim. 2:12, I Pet. 4:13* [5]*Luke 24:26* [6]*II Cor. 4:6, 11:23-30*
[7]*Matt. 20:23, John 18:11* [8]*Romans 8:18* [9]*Acts 9:16*
[10]*Acts 5:41* [11]*Matthew 16:24* [12]*Acts 16:2*

The Third Book

On Internal Consolation

Chapter 1

On Christ's Speaking Inwardly to a Faithful Soul

"I will hear what God the Lord will speak within me."[1]
Blessed is the soul who hears Jesus speaking in it and receives from His mouth some word of comfort.[2]

Blessed are the ears that hear the divine whispers, and give no heed to the deceitful whisperings of the world.[3]

Blessed indeed are the ears that do not heed the voice which is sounding outside, but listen to the truth which God speaks inwardly.

Blessed are the eyes that are shut to outward vanities but are intent on things within.

Blessed are they who enter into things internal, and endeavor to prepare themselves daily to receive more and more the hidden inspirations and inward teachings of God.

Blessed are they who seek to give their whole time to serve God and who rid themselves of every worldly hindrance.

2. Consider these things, O my soul, and shut the doors of your sensual desires, that you may hear what the Lord your God will speak within you.

Thus says your Beloved: I am your salvation, I am your peace, I am your life. Abide with Me and you will find peace.

Let go all transitory things and seek the things eternal.

What are all temporal things but deceitful? And what can all things avail you if you are forsaken by your Creator?

Put away, then, all other things, and make yourself pleasing to your Creator and be faithful to Him, so that after this life you may attain true blessedness.

[1]*Psalm 85:8* [2]*Psalm 94:12,13* [3]*Matthew 13:16,17*

Chapter 2

How God Speaks Without Words

Speak, Lord, for Your servant hears."[1]

"I am your servant: give me understanding that I may know Your testimonies."[2]

Incline my heart to the words of Your mouth: let Your speech distill as the dew.

In times past the children of Israel said to Moses, "Speak to us and we will hear; let not the Lord speak to us lest we die."[3]

Not so, Lord, not so do I pray. Rather with the prophet Samuel I humbly and earnestly entreat, "Speak, Lord, for Your servant hears."

Let not Moses speak to me, nor any of the prophets, but rather do You speak, O Lord God, the inspirer and giver of light to all the prophets. You alone without them can perfectly instruct me. They without You can profit me nothing.

2. They indeed speak forth words, but they cannot give the Spirit.

They speak most beautifully, but if You are silent, they cannot kindle the heart.

They teach the letter, but You open the sense; they bring forth mysteries, but You open the true understanding of their signs.

They declare the commandments, but You enable us to obey them.

They show the way, but You give the strength to walk in it.

They work from outside, but You instruct and enlighten within the heart.

They water, but You give the increase.

They cry aloud in words, but You give understanding of the words that are heard.

3. Let not Moses, then, speak to me, but You, O Lord, Eternal God, lest I die and prove unfruitful, warned outwardly but not enkindled within; lest the word rise up in judgment against me which I have heard and not fulfilled, known and not loved, believed and not observed.

Speak, then, Lord, for Your servant hears, for You have the words of eternal life.[4]

Speak to me to the comfort of my soul, for the amendment of my whole life, to Your praise, glory, and everlasting honor.

[1] *I Samuel 3:9* [2] *Psalm 119:125* [3] *Exodus 20:19* [4] *John 6:68*

Chapter 3

On Hearing God's Word with Humility

My son, hear My words, words of greatest sweetness, far surpassing the knowledge of the philosophers and wise men of this world.

"My words are spirit and life,"[1] and cannot be fully comprehended by man's understanding.

They are not to be perverted for vain conceit, but are to be heard in silence and received with great humility and great affection of the heart.

Blessed is the man, O Lord, whom You instruct and

teach out of Your law, that You may give him rest in the evil days, that he will not be left desolate on this earth.

2. I taught the prophets from the beginning (says the Lord), yet I do not cease to speak to every creature even to this day; but many are hardened and are deaf to My voice.

Most men listen more gladly to the world than to God; they would rather follow the desires of the flesh than the good pleasure of God.

The world promises temporal things of small value, and yet it is served with great eagerness. I promise things most high and eternal, and yet the hearts of men remain slow and dull.

Who is there who serves and obeys me in all things with such care as the world and its rulers are served and obeyed? "Be ashamed, O Sidon," says the sea![2] And do you ask why this is?

For a little reward a long journey is undertaken; for eternal life many will hardly lift one foot from the ground.

The most pitiful reward is sought after; for a single penny sometimes there is shameful contention, for a slight promise or a little trifle men do not hesitate to toil day and night.

3. But, alas for sorrow! For an unchangeable good, for a reward all price beyond, for the highest honor, for glory which has no end they grudge the least fatigue.

Be ashamed, then, slothful and complaining servant, that they are more ready for the labor of death than you are for the labor of life.

They rejoice more in seeking vanity than you do in seeking the truth.

They are often disappointed in that in which they hope, but My promise deceives no man, and sends none empty away who trusts in Me.[3]

What I have promised, I will give, and what I have said, I will fulfill, if only a man remain faithful in My love even to the end.

I am the rewarder of all good men[4] and the strong approver of all the devout.[5]

A Prayer for the Grace of Devotion

5. 0 Lord my God! You are all my good. And who am I that I presume to speak to You? I am the poorest and most worthless of Your servants, a wretched worm, much poorer and more contemptible than I know or dare express.

Yet remember, Lord, that I am nothing, I have nothing, and can do nothing.

You alone are good, just, and holy; You can do all things, You give all things, leaving only the sinner empty.

Remember Your mercies, and fill my heart with Your grace, for You do not will that Your works should be in vain.

6. How can I bear the miseries of this life unless You give me strength by Your mercy and grace in it?

Do not turn Your face away from me.[6]

Do not delay Your visitation, nor withdraw Your consolation, lest my soul become a dry, thirsty land.

Teach me, O Lord, to do Your will.[7] Teach me to walk worthily and humbly before You. For You are my wisdom; You know me in truth, and knew me before the world was made and long before I was born into the world.

[1]*John 6:63* [2]*Cf. Isaiah 23:4* [3]*Romans 7:24*
[4]*Rev. 2:23, Matt. 5:6, 25:21* [5]*Cf. John 12:48* [6]*Psalm 69:17*
[7]*Psalm 143:10*

Chapter 4

On Walking Before God in Truth and Humility

My son, walk before Me in truth and always seek Me in the singleness of your heart.[1]

He who walks before Me in truth will be safe from the assaults of evil and the truth will set him free[2] from seducers and from the malice of the wicked.

"If the truth makes you free, you will be free indeed" and will not care for the vain words of men.

O Lord, it is true! As You say, so let it be with me, I pray. Let the truth teach me, guard me, and preserve me to the end.

Let it set me free from all evil affection and from all inordinate love, and I will walk with you in great liberty of heart.

2. I will teach you (says the Truth) what is acceptable and pleasing in My sight.

Reflect on your sins with great displeasure and sorrow of heart, and never consider yourself to be anything because of your good works.

In truth you are a sinner, you are subject to and entangled with many passions. Of yourself you always tend to nothingness. You soon fall, are quickly overcome, quickly disturbed, quickly unnerved.

You have nothing in which to glory[3] but many things for which you should consider yourself vile, for you are much weaker than you are able to comprehend.

3. Let nothing you do, then, seem great, nothing precious or wonderful, nothing worthy of esteem, nothing high,

nothing truly commendable or desirable except what is eternal.

Let the eternal truth please you above all things; let your own utter vileness always displease you.

Fear nothing so much, blame nothing so much as your own vices and sins, which ought to be more displeasing to you than any loss whatsoever of goods.

Some do not walk before me in sincerity, but being led by curiosity and pride, they desire to know My secret things and to understand the deep things of God, while they neglect themselves and their salvation.

These often fall into great temptations and sins through their pride and curiosity when I resist them.

Fear the judgments of God. Tremble before the wrath of the Almighty. Shrink from searching out the works of the Most High, but search narrowly into your own iniquities, into how many ways you have offended, and how much good you have neglected.

There are some who carry their devotion only in books, some in pictures, some in outward signs and figures.

Some have me on their lips, but little in their heart.

There are others who, enlightened in their understanding and purified in their affection, always long after eternal things, hear of earthly things with reluctance, and obey the necessities of nature with sorrow. And these feel what the Spirit of Truth speaks in them.

For He teaches them to despise the things of the earth, to love heavenly things, to disregard the world, and to desire Heaven all the day and night.

[1]*Genesis 17:1* [2]*John 8:31* [3]*I Corinthians 4:7*

Chapter 5

On the Wonderful Effect of Divine Love

I bless You, Heavenly Father, Father of my Lord Jesus Christ, for You have vouchsafed to remember me, a poor creature.

Father of mercies and God of all comfort, I thank You that You sometimes refresh me, unworthy as I am, with Your comfort.

I bless You and glorify You continually with Your only-begotten Son and the Holy Spirit, the Paraclete, forever and ever.

O Lord my God, holy lover of my soul, when You come into my heart, all that is within me rejoices. You are my glory, the joy of my heart. You are my hope and my refuge in the day of troubles.

2. But because I am as yet weak in love and imperfect in virtue, I need Your strength and consolation. Visit me often, then, and instruct me with holy discipline.

Set me free from all evil passions, and heal my heart of all inordinate affections, that being inwardly healed and thoroughly cleansed, I may be made fit to love, strong to suffer, and steady to persevere.

3. Love is a great good, a great good indeed; by itself it makes everything light that is burdensome and it makes the rough places smooth.

It bears a burden without being burdened, and it makes all that is bitter sweet and pleasant.

The ennobling love of Jesus impels to great things and stirs us up to desire to greater perfection.

Love tends upward and refuses to be held down by even the lowest and meanest.

Love desires to be free from all worldly affections, so that the soul's inward vision may not be dimmed or hindered, so that it may not be entangled by temporal prosperity nor overcome by adversity.

Nothing is sweeter than love, nothing stronger, nothing higher, nothing broader, nothing more pleasant, nothing fuller nor better in Heaven or on earth, because love is born of God and cannot rest finally in anything lower than God.

4. One who loves, flies, runs, and rejoices; he is free and untrammeled.

He gives all for all and has all in all, because he rests in the One who is highest above all, from whom all good flows and proceeds.

He does not look for gifts, but turns himself to the Giver above all good things.

Love often knows no measure, but breaks out above measure.

Love feels no burden, regards no labor, attempts what is beyond its strength, pleads no excuse of impossibility, for it thinks it can and may do all things.

Love, therefore, does many great things and achieves them where he who does not love faints and lies down.

5. Love is watchful, and sleeping, slumbers not.

Weary, it is not exhausted; pressed, it is not constrained; alarmed, it is not terrified. Like a lively flame or a burning torch, it forces its way upward and safely triumphs.

If anyone loves, he knows well the cry of the voice–it is a loud cry in the ears of God, that ardent affection which cries, "O Lord my God, You are my whole love and desire. You are all mine and I am all Yours."

6. Enlarge me in love, that with my inward heart I may taste how sweet it is to love and to be dissolved and bathed in a sea of love.

Let me be possessed by love, rising above my self in fervor and adoration.

Let me sing the song of love and I shall follow You, my Beloved, on high. Let my soul spend itself in Your praise, rejoicing greatly in love.

Let me love You more than myself, and myself only for You, and all in You who truly love You, as the law of love, which shines from You, commands.

7. Love is swift, sincere, pious, pleasant, and strong; it is patient, faithful, longsuffering, manly, and never self-seeking.[1]

For wherever a man is self-seeking, there he falls from love.[2]

Love is circumspect, humble, and upright, not soft, not fickle, not intent on vain things. It is sober, chaste, steady, quiet, keeping guard over all the senses.

Love is submissive and obedient to superiors, and in its own sight of little worth and despicable. To God it is thankful and devout, ever trusting and hoping always in Him, even when it does not sense God's presence, for no one lives in love without some sorrow and pain.

8. Whoever is not ready to suffer and to stand fully at the bidding of his Beloved is not worthy to be called a lover of God.

He who loves ought to embrace willingly all that is hard and distasteful for the sake of his Beloved, and must not turn away from Him on account of any adversity that may befall him.

[1]*I Corinthians 13:5* [2]*I Corinthians 10:33, Philippians 2:21*

Chapter 6

On the Proof of a True Lover

My son, you are not yet a strong and wise lover.

Why, Lord?

Because at a little adversity or opposition you abandon what you have undertaken and too greedily seek some outward consolation.

A valiant and faithful lover of God stands fast in temptations and does not yield to the crafty persuasions of the enemy. As I please him in prosperity, so I do not displease him in adversity.

2. A prudent lover does not consider the gift so much as he does the love of the Giver.

He looks more at the good will than the value of the gift and prizes all gifts little in comparison with his Beloved who gives them to him.

A noble lover does not rest in the gift, but in Me above every gift.

All is not lost, then, if you sometimes feel less devotion to Me and to My saints than you would like to feel.

That good and sweet affection which you sometimes feel is the effect of present grace, a sort of foretaste of your heavenly home; but it is not good to lean too much on such comforts, for they come and go.

Always to strive, however, against evil thoughts which arise in your mind, and to despise all the suggestions of the enemy, is a token of virtue and of great merit.

3. Do not let strange fancies trouble you, on whatever subject they may crowd into your mind. Keep your resolution with courage and persevere in your upright intention towards God.

It is not an illusion that you are sometimes suddenly lifted into ecstasy, only to be quickly returned to the usual vain thoughts of your heart.

For you suffer such trivialities rather against your will than with your consent, and therefore, if you are displeased with them, it will be to your merit rather than loss.

4. Know that the ancient foe, the devil, will try by all means to hinder your desire to good and to divert you from every religious exercise if he can, especially from the reverent contemplation of the saints, from devout remembrance of My Passion, from the profitable recollection of your sins, from keeping guard of your heart, and from the steadfast purpose to advance in godliness.

He suggests many evil thoughts, so that he may weary and discourage you from holy reading and prayer.

He cannot bear humble confession, and if he could he would cause you to cease from communion.

Do not believe him or listen to him, no matter how often he sets his traps of deceit to ensnare you.

Make all his malice return to himself again when he suggests wicked and unclean thoughts. Say to him:

"Get away from me, you wicked and unclean spirit! Blush, you miserable wretch! You are foul indeed to bring such a thought into my mind.

"Away with you, you wicked seducer! You shall have no part in me, but JESUS shall be with me as a valiant Warrior, and you shall stand confounded!

"I had rather die and undergo any torment than consent to you!

"Hold your peace and be silent! I will not listen any more

to you, even though you trouble me ever so much. 'The Lord is my light and my salvation; whom shall I fear?'[1]

" 'Though a host should encamp against me, my heart shall not be afraid.'[2] 'The Lord is my helper and redeemer.' "[3]

5. Fight like a good soldier.[4] And if through your frailty you sometimes fall, rise up with greater strength than before, trusting in My more abundant grace. But guard yourself beforehand against complacency and pride!

Pride brings many into error and into such blindness of soul, that it becomes almost incurable.

Let the fall of the proud who presume on their own strength serve as a warning to you to keep you ever humble.

[1]*Psalm 27:1* [2]*Psalm 27:3* [3]*Psalm 19:14* [4]*Psalm 27:14, I Timothy 6:12*

CHAPTER 7

On Hiding Grace in Humility

My son, it is much better and safer for you to hide the grace of devotion and not to be elevated by it, not to speak much of it nor dwell greatly on it, but rather to despise yourself the more and to consider yourself unworthy of any such gracious gift of God.

It is not good to cleave much to such feelings as may so quickly change to the opposite.

When you have grace, think how wretched you are without it.

Your progress in the spiritual life does not so much consist in having this grace. Rather it is in enduring its withdrawal with humility, resignation, and patience, so that you do not then become careless in prayer or neglectful of the rest of your accustomed duties.

Do cheerfully what you are able to do according to the best of your ability and understanding, and take care not to neglect yourself because of the dryness or anxiety of mind which you experience.

2. There are many who, when things do not go well for them, become impatient or slothful.

For the way of man is not always in his power,[1] but it belongs to God to give and to comfort when He wills, as much as He wills, and to whom He wills; as it shall please Him and no more.

Some unwise persons, in their over-eager desire for the grace of devotion, have destroyed themselves; because they attempted more than they were able to carry out, not knowing the measure of their own weakness, following the inclination of their own heart rather than the dictates of reason.

Because they presumptuously undertook greater things than were pleasing to God, they quickly lost grace.

They were left needy and wretched, who had thought to build themselves nests in Heaven itself,[2] so that, being humbled and impoverished, they might learn not to fly with their own wings but to trust under Mine.

They who are yet but new and inexperienced in the way of the Lord, unless they govern themselves by the counsel of the wise, may easily be deceived and broken to pieces.

3. If they follow their own notions instead of trusting others who are more experienced, it will be very perilous for them in the end, if they are unwilling to be drawn away from their own conceit.

It is very rare that they who are wise in their own sight are willing to be ruled or ordered by others.

It is better to have little knowledge with humility than to have great treasures of learning with vain self-conceit.[3]

It is better for you to have little, than to have much of that which may make you proud.

He does not act discreetly who gives himself wholly to gladness and mirth, forgetting his former desolation and that chastened fear of the Lord which is afraid of losing the grace already given.

Nor is he wise who, in time of adversity or heaviness, at once gives in to despair and does not feel or think of Me as trustfully as he should.

4. He who is overly secure in time of peace will often be found too greatly dejected and full of fears in time of battle and temptation.[4]

If you knew how to remain humble and little in your own sight, and could order well the emotions of your own soul, you would not so quickly fall into danger and offenses.

It is good counsel, that when you have this intensity of feeling kindled in your spirit, you should think how it will be with you when that fervor is past.

And when that fervor does leave you, then remember that it may return again, which as a warning to you and for My own glory I have withdrawn for a time.

5. It is better for you to be so tried than that you should always have things prosper according to your will.

A man's worthiness is not to be estimated by the number of visions and consolations he may have, by his skill in the Scriptures, nor by his high position.

Rather, he is worthy who is securely grounded in humility and full of divine love, who is always simply and sincerely seeking God's honor, who esteems himself nothing and truly despises himself, even preferring to be despised and humiliated by others than to be honored by them.

[1]*Jer. 10:23, Rom. 9:16* [2]*Isaiah 14:13* [3]*Ps. 16:2, 17:10* [4]*I Thess. 5:6*

Chapter 8

On Thinking Humbly of Ourselves Before God

Shall I speak to my Lord, though I am but dust and ashes? If I think anything better of myself, You stand against me and my own sins bear witness that I cannot deny.

But if I abase myself and set myself at nought, and think myself but dust and ashes as I am, then Your grace will draw near me, and Your light will enter my heart, and all pride and presumption in me will be drowned in the depth of humility and perish forever.

There You reveal to me what I am, what I have been, and whence I have come, for I am nothing and knew it not.

If I am left to myself, I am nothing but mere weakness. But if for an instant You look on me, I am quickly made strong and filled with new joy.

It is great marvel indeed that I am so suddenly lifted up and so graciously embraced by You—I who always sink downward of my own weight.

2. It is Your love that causes all this, going before me and helping me in a multitude of necessities, guarding me from pressing dangers and snatching me (as I can truly say) from evils out of number.

For by an evil loving of myself amiss, I lost myself; and by seeking You and sincerely loving You alone, I have found both myself and You, and by that love You have even more deeply reduced me to nothing.

O Most Dear Jesus, You deal with me above all I deserve and above all that I dare or desire.

3. You are blessed, O my God, in all Your works, for though I am unworthy of all good, yet Your generosity and infinite goodness never cease to do good even to the ungrateful who are turned away from You.

Turn us to You, that we may be thankful, humble, and devout; for You are our salvation, our courage, and our strength.

Chapter 9

On Referring All Things to God

My son, I must be your supreme and ultimate end if you would be truly happy.

By this intention your affections will be purified, which are too often inordinately inclined to yourself and to other creatures.

If you seek yourself in anything as the end of your work, you wither away in yourself and become dry and barren.

I would that you should refer all things to Me first of all, for I have given all to you.

So look upon everything as flowing from the Supreme Good, and therefore everything is to be attributed to me as its original Source.

2. From me the small and the great, the rich and the poor draw the water of life,[1] as from a living fountain. They who willingly and freely serve Me shall receive grace for grace.

But he who desires to glory in things apart from Me, or willfully joy in anything besides Me, will not be grounded in true joy nor enlarged in his heart. He will be hindered in many ways and thrown into tribulation.

Ascribe no goodness to yourself nor attribute goodness

to any man, but ascribe all goodness to God, without whom man has nothing.

I have given all, and I will have all returned to Me again. With great strictness do I require of you a return of thanks.

3. This is the truth by which all vainglory and pride of heart are put to flight.

If heavenly grace and true love come into you, there will be no envy or narrowness of heart, nor will self-love rule in you.

The love of God overcomes all things and expands all the powers of the soul.

If you are truly wise, you will never rejoice but in Me, in Me alone will you hope; for none is good but God alone,[2] who is to be honored above all things, and in all things to be blessed.

[1]*John 4:14* [2]*Matthew 19:17, Luke 18:9*

Chapter 10

On the Sweetness of God's Service

Now I will speak again, Lord, and will not be silent. I will say in the hearing of my God, my Lord and my King, who dwells on high: "O how abundant is Thy goodness, which Thou hast laid up for those who fear Thee!"[1]

But what are You to those who love You? What to those who serve You with their whole heart?

Truly unspeakable is the sweetness of that vision of You which You give to those who love You.

In this especially You have shown me the sweetness of Your love, that when I had no being, You made me, and when I was far astray from You, You brought me back again to serve You; and You bid me to love You.

2. O Fountain of ever-flowing love, what shall I say to You?

How can I forget You who deigned to remember me?

When I was wasted away and lost, You showed Your mercy to me above all that I could think and desire, and bestowed Your grace and love beyond all deserving.

What return shall I make to You for this grace?[2] It is not granted to all to forsake the world and to take the monastic life.

Is it any great thing that I should serve You[3] whom every creature is bound to serve?

It ought not to seem any great thing to me to serve You, but rather it should seem a marvel and a wonder to me that You would receive such a poor and unworthy creature as I am into Your service, and that You will make him one of Your chosen servants.

3. Behold, all are Yours. Everything that I have, and all with which I do You service are Yours.[4]

And yet, on the other hand, it is You who serve me rather than I, You.

For lo, the heavens and the earth which You created to serve man, are ready at Your bidding and daily do that which You have commanded.

You have also appointed angels for the service of man.[5]

But above all this, You Yourself have deigned to serve man, and have promised to give Yourself to him.

4. What shall I give You for all these thousandfold benefits? Would that I might serve You all the days of my life!

Would that I could at least for one day do You some worthy service!

Truly You are worthy of all honor, all service and praise forever.

Truly You are my Lord, and I am Your poor servant, most bound before all others to love You and praise You, and I should never grow weary of praising You.

This I ask and this I desire. Vouchsafe, therefore, most merciful Lord, to supply what is lacking in me.

5. It is a great honor and a great glory to serve You and to despise all earthly things for the sake of loving You.

They will have great grace who freely submit themselves to Your most holy service.

They who here forsake all carnal delight out of love for You shall find the most sweet consolation of the Holy Spirit. They shall have great freedom of spirit who for Your name's sake enter upon a narrow way and lay aside all worldly care.

6. O pleasant and delightful service of God, by which a man is made truly free and holy!

O holy state of religious service, which makes a man like the angels, pleasing to God and dreadful to wicked spirits, worthy to be commended by all the faithful.

O service worthy to be desired, and ever to be chosen, by which the supreme good is won and everlasting joy and gladness attained that will abide without end!

[1]*Psalm 31:19a* [2]*Psalm 116:12* [3]*Luke 17:10*
[4]*I Corinthians 4:7* [5]*Psalm 91:11, Hebrews 1:14*

Chapter 11

On the Devices and Desires of the Heart

My son, you still have many things to learn which you have not yet learned well.

2. What are they, Lord?

3. That you must conform your desires in all things to My good pleasure, and that you should not be a lover of yourself, but be earnestly zealous that My will be done.

Various desires often inflame you and drive you violently headlong; consider whether you are being moved by your self-interest rather than for My honor.

If I am your motivation, you will be well contented with whatever I ordain. But if there is lurking in you any self-seeking, this will hinder you and weigh you down.

4. Beware, then, that you do not lean too much on any desire conceived without asking My counsel, lest afterward you are sorry and displeased with that which pleased you formerly and which you earnestly sought as the best.

Not every impulse which seems good is to be heeded immediately, nor, on the other hand, is every contrary feeling at once to be avoided.

It is well to check yourself at times, even in good desires and endeavors, lest through too much eagerness you should become distracted in mind, or by lack of self-control you create a scandal to others; or again, facing opposition or resistance by others, you become suddenly confounded and so fall.

5. In some cases you must use violence[1] and manfully resist the sensual appetite, paying no heed to what the

flesh would or would not;[2] but rather taking pains that even against its will, it be made subject to the spirit.

Moreover, it should be chastened and kept under control until it is prepared for all things, to be pleased with plain and simple things, and not to murmur at any inconvenience.

[1] *I Corinthians 9:27* [1] *Romans 8:1-13, II Corinthians 4:10, 10:3*

Chapter 12

On Patient Wrestling Against Carnal Desires

O Lord God, I see that patience is very necessary for me,[1] for many things in this life do not happen as we would like.

I see well that whatever plans I make for my own peace, my life cannot be without some battle and sorrow.[2]

It is so, My son. But My will is not that you seek to have such peace as to be without temptations or to be without opposition. Rather think that you have found peace when you are exercised with many troubles and tried with many things that go against you in this world.

2. If you say you are not able to suffer so much, how then will you be able to suffer the fire of purgatory?[3]

Of two evils we should always choose the lesser. Strive, then, on God's behalf to endure the little pains of this world, so that you may escape eternal torments in the world to come.

Do you think that the men of this world suffer little or nothing? Ask even the most pampered and you will find it otherwise.

3. But you will say, that they have many delights, and follow their own wills, and that they think but little of all their tribulations.

4. Well, even if that is so, that they have whatever they desire, how long do you think it will last?

Behold, they who abound in this world shall suddenly vanish away as smoke[4] and there will be left no remembrance of their past joys!

And yes, even while they are living, they are not without great bitterness, weariness, and fear.

For from the very thing in which they delight they often receive the penalty of sorrow and pain.

And it is only just that having inordinately sought and followed after their pleasures, that they should not enjoy them without shame and bitterness.

O how short, how deceitful, how inordinate and base are all those pleasures!

Yet through sottishness and blindness of heart, men do not understand it. Like dumb beasts they incur the death of their souls for a small pleasure in this corruptible life.

Therefore, my son, "go not after your lusts, but turn away from your will."[5] "Delight yourself in the Lord and He will give you the desires of your heart."[6]

5. If you desire true delights and plentiful consolations from Me, you will find them in the contempt of all worldly things and in cutting off all inordinate desires; then you will be blessed with the abundant comfort of God.

The more you withdraw yourself from the consolation of creatures, the more sweet and blessed consolations you will find in Me.

But at first, you will experience some sadness, some heaviness and labor in order to attain them.

An old inbred habit will resist, but by a better habit, it will be overcome.

The flesh will murmur, but by the fervor of spirit it shall be restrained.

The old serpent will tempt you if he can, but by prayer he will be put to flight, and by useful work you will greatly block a main approach of his.

[1]*Hebrews 10:36* [2]*Job 7:1*

[3]Unlike many English versions, we have chosen to allow references such as these to remain as the author wrote them.

[4]*Psalm 68:2* [5]*Ecclesiasticus 18:30* [6]*Psalm 37:4*

Chapter 13

On Humble Obedience, After the Example of Jesus Christ

Son, he who endeavors to withdraw himself from obedience, withdraws himself from grace. He who seeks private privileges for himself,[1] loses those which are common to all.

Whoever does not freely and spontaneously submit himself to his superior shows that his flesh is not as yet perfectly brought into submission, and that it often rebels and murmurs.

Learn then, to submit yourself to your superior if you desire to subdue your own flesh.

For the outward enemy is more speedily overcome if the inward man is not in disarray.

There is no worse enemy nor a more troublesome one to the soul than you are to yourself when not at peace with the Spirit.

It is altogether necessary that you have a true contempt of yourself if you desire to prevail over your flesh and blood.

2. Because you still love yourself inordinately, you are afraid to resign your will wholly to the will of others.

Yet, what great matter is it for you, who are but dust and nothing, to submit yourself to man for God's sake, when I, the Almighty and Most High Maker of all things, humbly subjected Myself to man for your sake?

I became the most humble and lowest of all, that you should learn to overcome your pride by my humility.

O dust! Learn to obey! Learn to humble yourself, O earth and clay! And to bow yourself down under the feet of all.

Learn to break your own will and to yield yourself to all subjection.

3. Rise in great wrath against yourself, and do not allow pride to reign in you. Show yourself so humble and lowly that all may be able to walk over you, to tread you down as the mire of the streets. O vain man! Of what do you have to complain?

What can you answer, vile sinner, to those who reproach you, you who have so often offended God and so many times have deserved hell?

But nevertheless, My eye has spared you, for your soul is precious in My sight; that you might know my love and ever be thankful for My benefits.

And again, that you might give yourself continually to true submission and humility, and bear with patience your share of contempt. Amen.

[1]*Matthew 16:24*

Chapter 14

On the Secret and Hidden Judgments of God

Lord, You thunder forth Your judgments over me; You shake all my bones with fear and trembling, and my soul is greatly terrified.

I stand amazed when I consider that even the heavens are not pure in Your sight.[1]

If you found wickedness in the angels[2] and did not spare them, what shall become of me?

Even stars fell from Heaven! And I, who am but dust, how can I presume?

There were some, too, whose works seemed great and commendable who fell into the very lowest, and those who had eaten the bread of angels,[3] I have seen delighting in the husks of swine.

2. There is then no holiness, Lord, if You withdraw Your hand.

No wisdom avails us if You cease to govern.

No strength helps if You cease to uphold us.

No chastity is secure if You do not protect it.

No vigilance of our own avails if Your holy watchfulness is not over us.[4]

If we are forsaken by You, we sink and perish. Visited by You, we are raised up and live.

We are unstable indeed unless You establish us; we are lukewarm unless we are set on fire by You.

3. O how humbly and abjectly ought I to reckon myself; and how greatly should I despise myself, though I seem ever so good and holy.

With what profound humility ought I to submit myself to

Your deep and unfathomable judgments, O Lord, since I find myself to be nothing else than nothing and very nothing!

O weight beyond measure ! O sea impassable! where I discover nothing about myself but nothing and totally nothing.

Where then can boasting hide itself? Where can be my confidence in my own self-conceived virtue?

All vaingloryings is swallowed up in the depths of Your judgments upon me!

4. What is all flesh in Your sight?

Shall the clay boast against Him that formed it?

How can he be lifted up with vain talk whose heart is truly subjected to God?[5]

All the world cannot move him to pride, whom the truth has subjected to itself; neither shall he be moved by the tongues of all who praise him, whose whole hope is firmly settled in God.

For he sees well that even those who speak are themselves nothing, for they shall all pass away with the sound of their words. But the truth of the Lord shall endure forever.[6]

[1]*Job 15:15* [2]*Job 4:18* [3]*Psalm 78:25*
[4]*Psalm 127:1* [5]*Isaiah 29:16* [6]*Psalm 117:2*

Chapter 15

On Dealing with Our Desires

Son, in everything you desire, say, "Lord, if this is pleasing to You, let it be so.

"Lord, if it be to Your honor, let this be done in Your name.

"Lord, if You see this is good and expedient for me, give me grace to use it to Your honor.

"But if You know it will be hurtful to me and not expedient to the health of my soul, then take from me such desire."[1]

For not every good desire proceeds from the Holy Spirit, even though such seem good and right to a man.

It is difficult to judge truly whether it be a good spirit or an evil one which is urging you to desire this or that, or whether you are moved by your own spirit.

Many have been deceived in the end, who at first seemed to be moved by a good spirit.

2. Therefore, whatever seems desirable must always be desired and prayed for in the fear of God and with humility of heart, with a whole resignation of yourself to commit all things to Me; and you must say, "Lord, you know what way is best. Let this or that be done as You please.

"Give what You will and as much as You will and when You will.

"Do with me as You know best, as best pleases You and is most for Your honor.

"Put me where You will and freely do with me in all things just as You will.

"I am in Your hands. Lead me and turn me where You will.

"Lo, I am Your servant, ready to do everything that You command, for I desire to live, not to myself, but to You.

"Would that I could do it worthily and perfectly."

A Prayer that the Will of God May Be Fulfilled

3. O most benign Jesus, grant me Your grace, that it may be with me and work with me and continue with me to the end.

Grant me always to desire and will that which is most acceptable and most pleasing to You.

Let Your will be mine, and let my will always follow Your will and agree perfectly with it.

Let my will be always one with Yours, and let me have no power to will or not will, except as You will or will not.

4. Grant that I may die to all things that are in the world, and for Your sake, may I love to be despised and to be unknown in this world.

Grant to me above all things that I can desire, that I may rest in You, and have my heart at peace in You.

For You are the true peace of the heart; You its only rest; out of You all things are hard and restless. In this peace that is in You alone, the one sovereign, eternal Good, "I will lay me down and take my rest."[2] Amen.

[1]*I Corinthians 6:12* [2]*Psalm 4:8*

Chapter 16

On Seeking True Comfort in God Alone

Whatever I can desire or imagine for my comfort, I look for it not here, but hereafter.

If I should possess all the comforts of the world and might enjoy all its delights,[1] it is certain that they could not long endure.

Therefore my soul cannot be fully comforted nor have complete refreshment, except in God, the Comforter of the poor, and the Helper of the humble.

Wait a little while, O my soul; wait for the divine promise

and you will have an abundance of all the goodness of Heaven.

If you desire inordinately the things of this present time, you will lose those which are heavenly and eternal.

Use present things, and *desire* heavenly ones.

You cannot be fully satisfied by any temporal good, because you are not created to rest in them.

2. Although you should possess all created goods, you could not be happy or blessed thereby. Only in God, who created all things, consist your whole blessedness and happiness.[2]

That happiness is not such as seems good to the foolish lovers of this world, but such as the good and faithful servants of Christ wait for and of which the spiritual and pure in heart, whose "conversation is in Heaven,"[3] sometimes taste here in this present life.

All human solace is vain and short-lived.

Blessed and true is that solace which is received inwardly from the truth.

A devout man bears about with him everywhere his own comforter, Jesus, and says to Him, "Be present with me, Lord Jesus, in every place and time.

"Let this be my comfort, to be willing to lack all human solace.

"And if Your consolation is withdrawn, let Your will and Your just trial of me be to me as the greatest comfort; for You will not always be angry, neither will You chide forever."[4]

[1]*Matthew 16:26* [2]*Wisdom 2:23* [3]*Philippians 3:20* [4]*Psalm 103:9*

Chapter 17

On Resting All Our Cares Upon God

Son, allow Me to do with you what I will, for I know what is best and most expedient for you.

You think as a man. In many things you judge as human affection suggests.

O Lord! What you say is true. Your care for me is greater[1] than all the care I can take of myself.

For he stands too insecurely who does not cast all his care on You.

If only my will remain right and firm towards You, Lord, do with me whatever it pleases You.

For it cannot be anything but good, whatever You shall do with me.

2. If it is Your will that I should be in darkness, You are blessed. And if it is Your will that I should be in light, again You are blessed! If You choose to comfort me, You are blessed; and if You will that I should be afflicted, You are blessed also.

Son, this ought to be your state if you desire to walk with Me.

You must be as ready to suffer as to rejoice.

You must be as willing to be needy and poor as to be full and rich.

3. O Lord, for Your sake I will cheerfully suffer[2] whatever comes upon me with Your permission.

From Your hand I am willing to receive with indifference good and evil, sweet and bitter, joy and sorrow; and for all that befalls me, I will be thankful.

Keep me from all sin and I shall fear neither death[3] nor Hell.

No tribulation whatever that befalls me will hurt me if only You do not cast me from Your presence forever nor blot me out of the Book of Life.

[1]*Matthew 6:30* [2]*Job 2:10* [3]*Psalm 23:4*

Chapter 18

On Bearing Suffering Patiently

My son, I came down from Heaven[1] for your salvation; I took upon Myself your miseries, not out of necessity, but drawn by love, so that you yourself might learn patience, and bear temporal sufferings without complaint.

For from the hour of My birth[2] even until My death on the Cross, I was not free from grief and sorrow.

I endured great lack of temporal things; I often heard many complaints against Me; I endured patiently disgrace and reviling. In return for blessings, I received ingratitude; for My miracles, blasphemies; for My teaching, rebukes.

2. O Lord, since You were patient in Your lifetime, fulfilling especially in this way the will of Your Father,[3] it is fitting that I, a pitiful sinner, should bear myself patiently in everything according to Your will, and for the welfare of my soul, bear the burden of this corruptible life as long as You Yourself shall choose.

For although this present life seems burdensome, yet now by Your grace it has been made very purposeful, and by Your example and by the footsteps of Your saints, more bright and clear and more endurable to the weak.

It is also much more full of consolation than it was under the old Law, when the gate of Heaven was shut and the way to Heaven seemed darker, and so few cared to seek the kingdom of Heaven.[4]

And not even they who were then just and of the saved could enter into the kingdom of Heaven before the accomplishment of Your blessed Passion and Death.

3. O what great thanks I am bound to give You, because You have deigned to show to me and to all faithful people the good and right way to the eternal kingdom.

For Your life is our life, and by holy patience we walk on to You, our Crown.

If You had not gone before us and taught us, who would care to follow?

Alas, how many would remain behind afar off, if they did not have before their eyes Your glorious example!

We are even yet dull and slow, though we have heard of Your many miracles and teachings. What would become of us if we did not have so great a light by which to follow You?

[1]*John 3:13* [2]*Luke 2:7* [3]*John 5:30* [4]*Matthew 7:14*

Chapter 19

On Enduring Wrongs with True Patience

My son, what is it that you say? Stop complaining, as you consider My Passion and the sufferings of My other saints.

You have not yet resisted to the point of shedding your blood.[1]

That which you suffer is but little in comparison to those who have suffered so much, who were so strongly tempted, so grievously troubled, tried, and proved in so many ways.[2]

You ought to call to mind the greater sufferings of others, so you may the more easily endure your own very small troubles.

If they do not seem very small to you, then beware, lest your own impatience be the cause of them.

However, whether they are small or great, endeavor to bear them all with patience.

2. The better you can dispose yourself to suffer them, the more wisely you behave and the greater reward you earn. You will more easily endure it if both in mind and by habit you are diligently prepared for it.

Do not say, "I cannot endure to suffer these things at the hands of such a man, nor should I endure things of this kind! For he has done me great wrong and reproaches me with things which I never thought of; but I would willingly suffer from someone else as much as I think I ought to suffer."

Such a thought is foolish; it does not take into account the virtue of patience, and forgets by Whom it shall be crowned. Rather, it weighs too exactly the persons involved, and the injuries given to self.

3. He is not truly patient who will suffer only as much as he thinks is good and from whom he chooses.

The truly patient man does not consider by whom he is tried, whether by his superior, or an equal, or by an inferior; whether it be by a good and holy man, or by one who is perverse and unworthy.

But whenever any adversity or wrong happens to him, whatever it may be, from whomsoever, and however often it be, he takes it all thankfully as from the hand of God, and accounts it a great and rich gift and blessing.

For with God it is impossible that anything, however small, should pass without its reward, provided it is suffered for God's sake.

4. Be prepared to battle, then, if you desire to gain the victory.

Without a combat you cannot obtain the crown of patience.[3] If you are unwilling to suffer, you refuse to be crowned. But if you desire to be crowned, fight manfully, endure patiently.

Without labor we are not approaching rest, and without fighting we cannot reach the victory.

O Lord! May Your grace make possible to me what is impossible to me by nature. You know well that I can bear but little, and that I am quickly defeated by a slight adversity.

For Your name's sake, let any trouble and adversity hereafter be made pleasant and desirable to me, for to be troubled and to be harassed for You is very wholesome for my soul.

[1]*Hebrews 12:4* [2]*Hebrews 11:37* [3]*II Timothy 2:3-5*

Chapter 20

On Human Weakness and Misery

I will acknowledge my unrighteousness against myself,[1] and I will confess to You, Lord, my weakness.

Often it is but a little thing that makes me sad and dejected.

I resolve to behave myself valiantly, but when even a little temptation comes, I am in sore straits.

Sometimes it is a very small trifle out of which a grievous temptation springs.

And when I think that I am quite safe, when I least expect it, I sometimes find myself almost overcome by a slight puff of wind.

2. Behold, then, Lord, my humiliation and frailty, which are fully known to You in every way.[2]

Have mercy on me, and draw me out of the mire, that my feet may not stick fast in it, and that I may not be utterly cast down forever.[3]

This is what often strikes me down and confounds me in Your sight, that I am so prone to fall, and so weak in resisting my passions.

And although I do not always consent, yet their continual assaults are troublesome and grievous, and it is exceedingly taxing to live in this daily conflict.

Hence, I know better my own weakness, because such wicked imaginations always arise in me much more easily than they go away.

3. Most mighty God of Israel, zealous Lover of faithful souls! O that You would consider the labor and sorrow of Your servant, and would assist him in all things in which he strives!

Strengthen me with heavenly strength, lest the old man, the miserable flesh, which is not yet fully subdued to the spirit, should have dominion or get the upper hand over me. I will need to fight against it as long as I breathe in this miserable life.

Alas, what life is this, where tribulation and miseries are never lacking, where there are snares and mortal enemies at every turn?

For when one trouble or temptation goes away, another comes; yes, and while the first conflict is still raging, many others come on unexpectedly, one after another!

4. How can this life then be loved, which has such bitterness and is subject to so many miseries and calamities?

How can it be called *life* that brings forth so many deaths and plagues?

Yet it is loved and its delights are sought by many.

The world is often blamed for being deceitful and vain, yet men do not easily leave it, because the lusts of the flesh hold too much sway.

Some things stir a man to love the world, and some things, to despise it.

"The lust of the flesh, the lust of the eyes, and the pride of life"[4] stir a man to love the world.

But the pains and miseries that justly follow these things breed a hatred and a loathing of it.

5. But alas for sorrow! The fondness for impure pleasures overcomes the soul given to the world, and it thinks it a delight to be even under thorns,[5] because it has not seen or tasted the sweetness of God and the inward pleasures of virtue.

But they who perfectly despise the world and make it their aim to live for God under holy discipline experience the heavenly sweetness promised to those who truly forsake all. They see, too, how grievously mistaken the world is, and how grievously it is deceived in so many ways.

[1]*Psalm 32:5* [2]*Psalm 25:18* [3]*Psalm 49:14, 40:2*
[4]*I John 2:16* [5]*Job 30:7*

Chapter 21

On Resting Entirely in God

Above all things and in all things, my soul, rest in the Lord, for He is the eternal rest of all His saints.

Grant me, O most sweet and loving Lord Jesus, to rest in You, above all creatures,[1] above all health and beauty, above all glory and honor, above all dignity and power, above all knowledge and subtlety, above all riches and talent, above all joy and gladness, above all fame and praise, above all sweetness and consolation, above all hope and promise, above all merit and desire:

Above all gifts and rewards that You may give or impart, above all joy and jubilation that the mind or heart can contain and feel:

In a word, above angels and archangels, and above all the heavenly host, above all things visible and invisible, and above all that is not You, my God.

2. Because You, my Lord God, are of all things good, You alone most high, You alone most mighty, You alone most sufficient, the fullness of all things; You alone the most sweet, most comforting.

You alone are most lovely and loving, You only are most noble, You alone are most glorious above all things, in whom all good things in their perfection are, have been, and shall be.

Therefore, whatever you give me, or reveal or promise to me that is not Yourself is little and insufficient to me, as long as I do not see or fully enjoy You.

For surely my heart cannot truly rest or be entirely satisfied unless it rest in You, and rise above all gifts and all other creatures whatsoever.

3. O my most beloved spouse, Jesus Christ, most pure Lover and Ruler of all creation, who will give me the wings of true liberty that I might fly away and rest in You?[2]

O when shall it be fully granted me to consider in quietness of mind and to see how sweet You are, my Lord God?

When shall I recollect myself in You, that for reason of my love of You I may not feel myself, but You alone, above all feeling and measure, in a manner not known to everyone?[3]

But now I often sigh and bear my unhappiness with grief; because I meet with many evils in this vale of miseries, which often trouble, grieve, and overcloud me, often hinder and distract me, allure and entangle me, so that I cannot have free access to you, and cannot enjoy the sweet welcomings so readily granted to the blessed spirits.

Let my sighings and inward desires of my heart, with my many desolations on the earth, come before You.

4. O Jesus, the Light and Brightness of everlasting glory, solace of the pilgrim soul, before You my lips are without a voice and my very silence speaks to You.

How long does my Lord delay to come to me?

Let Him come to me, His poor servant, and make me glad. Let Him stretch forth His hand and deliver this miserable wretch from all anguish.

Come, come! For without You there will be no glad day nor hour; for You are my gladness and without You my table is barren and empty.

A wretched creature am I, and as it were, imprisoned and bound with fetters, till You give me the light of Your presence and restore me to liberty, and show a favorable and loving countenance to me.

5. Let others seek instead of you whatever they please; nothing else that I seek, nothing that I shall seek can please

me, but You, my God, my Hope, my eternal Salvation.

I will not hold my peace, nor cease to entreat You, until Your grace returns again and You speak inwardly to me.

BEHOLD, I am here. Behold, I come to you, because you have called on Me. Your tears and the desire of your soul, your humiliation and the contrition of your heart have inclined and brought Me to you.

And I said, Lord, I have called You and have desired to enjoy You, being ready to refuse all things for Your sake.

For you first stirred me to seek You.

Blessed are You, therefore, O Lord, that You have showed this goodness to me after the multitude of Your mercies.

6. What more can Your servant say in your presence, but to humble himself greatly before You, ever mindful of his own iniquity and vileness?

For there is none like You, Lord, among the wonders in Heaven or in earth.

Your works are good, Your judgments are true, and by Your Providence all things are governed.

Therefore to You, O Wisdom of the Father, be everlasting praise and glory. Let my mouth, my soul, and all Your creatures praise and bless You together.

[1]*Romans 8:19-22* [2]*Psalm 55:6* [3]*Daniel 10*

Chapter 22

On the Remembrance of God's Many Benefits

Open my heart, O Lord, to behold Your law, and teach me to walk in Your commandments.[1]

Grant me to understand Your will and to remember Your many blessings with great reverence and due consideration, so that I may from now on yield You fitting thanks.

I know and confess that I am not able to give You due thanks even for the least of Your mercies.

I am less than the least blessing You have given me, and when I consider Your majesty, its very greatness makes my spirit tremble with awe and dread.

2. All that we have in our soul and body, whatever we possess outwardly or inwardly, naturally or supernaturally, are Your benefits, and all show forth Your bounty, mercy, and goodness, from whom we have received all good things.

Although one may have received more, another less, nevertheless, all are Yours; and without You not even the least can be possessed.

He who has received more cannot glory in his own merits, nor boast himself above others nor despise those with less. For he is greater and better who attributes less to himself and who, in returning thanks, is more truly humble and devout.

He who holds himself vilest of all men and judges himself most unworthy is best prepared to receive greater blessings.

3. He who has received fewer gifts ought not to be downcast or grieved; nor should he envy those who are enriched

with greater ones. Rather let him turn his mind to You and highly praise Your goodness, because You bestow Your gifts so bountifully, so freely, and so willingly without respect of persons.

All things come of You, and therefore You are to be praised and blessed in all things.

You know what is best to be given to every person, and why one has less and another more. It is not for us to reason and discuss, but for You to judge, who know what is right for everyone.

4. For this reason, O Lord God, I even count it a great mercy not to have much of that which outwardly and in the opinion of men is counted worthy of glory and praise.

He who considers his own poverty and unworthiness should be so far from being grieved or sad or downcast on that account, but rather should take great comfort and great joy.

For You, O God, have chosen the poor and humble and the despised of this world for Yourself, to be Your intimate friends and servants.

Witness Your apostles themselves, whom You made princes over all the earth.[2]

Yet they lived in the world without complaint,[3] without malice or guile, so humbly and simply that they even rejoiced to suffer reproach for Your name.[4] And what the world abhors, they embraced with great affection.

5. When a man loves You and acknowledges Your blessings, nothing ought to give him such joy as Your will in him and the good pleasure of Your eternal appointment.

With this he should be so contented and comforted that he would willingly be the least, even though others would wish to be the greatest.

He would be as peaceable and contented in the lowest

place as in the highest, as willing to be a despised castaway of no name or reputation in the world, as to be preferred in honor before others, and to be greater in the world than they.

For Your will and the love of Your glory ought to be preferred above all things, and should comfort and please him more than all the blessings which You have given or shall give to him.

[1]*Psalm 119* [2]*Psalm 45:16* [3]*I Thessalonians 2:10* [4]*Acts 5:41*

Chapter 23

On Four Things that Bring Peace

Son, I will teach you the way of peace and true freedom.

2. Lord, I pray, do as You say, for this is delightful for me to hear.

3. Son, make this your aim, to do the will of another rather than your own.[1]

Always choose to have less rather than more.[2]

Always seek the lower place, to be under the authority of all.[3]

Always desire and pray that the will of God may be wholly fulfilled in you.[4]

Anyone who does this enters within the borders of peace and rest.

4. Lord, this short discourse of Yours contains much perfection.[5]

It is few in words, but full in meaning and abundant in fruit.

If I could faithfully keep it, I should not be so easily troubled.

For as often as I feel myself disturbed and discontent, I find that I have strayed from this teaching.

But You can do all things and always desire the progress of my soul. Increase Your grace in me, that I may be able to fulfill Your words and perfect my salvation.

A Prayer Against Evil Thoughts

5. O Lord my God, be not far from me. My God, make haste to help me![6] For vain thoughts have risen up against me, and great fears have troubled my soul.

How shall I pass through them unhurt? How shall I break them down?

6. I shall go before you, says the Lord, and humble the great ones of the earth. Then I will open the prison doors and show you hidden things in secret places.[7]

7. Lord, do as You say, and let all evil thoughts flee from before Your face.

Truly this is my hope and my one consolation, to fly to You in every trouble, to trust in You, inwardly to call on You, and patiently to await Your consolation.

A Prayer for Mental Illumination

8. Enlighten me, O good Jesus, with the brightness of Your inward light, and take away all darkness from my heart.

Take away the multitude of my wandering thought, and crush those temptations which so violently assail me.

Fight mightily for me and drive away those evil beasts, those enticing lusts of the flesh, and thus speak peace through Your strength. Then the abundance of Your praise may sound in the holy court which is a pure conscience.

Command the winds and storms. Say to the sea, "Be still," and to the north wind, "Blow not!" and there shall be a great calm.

9. Send out Your light and Your truth that they may shine on the earth,[8] for until You enlighten me, I am as earth that is empty and void.

Pour forth Your grace from above and water my heart with the dew of Heaven; send down the waters of devotion to wash the face of the earth, that it bring forth good and perfect fruit.

Lift up my mind, oppressed with the load of sins, and raise my whole desire towards heavenly things, so that having tasted the sweetness of things above, I may find it irksome even to think of things below.

10. Take me, and snatch me away from all the fleeting consolations of creatures; for no created thing can fully fill and satisfy my longing. Join me to Yourself with the inseparable bonds of love, for You alone suffice one who loves You, and without You the whole universe is but frivolity.

[1]*Matthew 26:39, John 5:30, 6:38*
[2]*I Corinthians 10:24*
[3]*Luke 14:10*
[4]*Matthew 6:10*
[5]*Matthew 5:48*
[6]*Psalm 71:12*
[7]*Isaiah 14:2, 3*
[8]*Psalm 43:3*

Chapter 24

On Inordinate Curiosity

Son, do not be curious nor trouble yourself with those things which do not belong to you.

What is this thing or that to you? Follow Me.[1]

What is it to you whether this man is good or bad, or whether he says or does this or that?

You will not need to answer for others, but you must give account of yourself. Why, then, do you entangle yourself?

Behold, I know everyone, and see everything that is done under the sun, and I understand how it is with everyone: what he thinks, what he wants, and what his intentions are.

Therefore, all these concerns are to be committed to Me; but, as for you, keep yourself in peace, and let the busybody be as busy as he will.

Whatever he shall do or say will come upon himself, for he cannot deceive Me.

2. Do not seek the shadow of a great name, or the familiar friendship of many, or the particular and exclusive affection of anyone.

For these things beget much unquietness of mind and will bring great darkness into your soul.

I would gladly speak My Word and reveal My secrets to you if you would diligently watch for My coming and open to Me the door of your heart.

Be circumspect and watchful in prayer, and humble yourself in all things.[2]

[1]*John 21:22* [2]*I Peter 4:7*

Chapter 25

On Peace of Heart and True Spiritual Progress

Son, I have said, peace I leave with you, My peace I give unto you; not as the world gives do I give to you.[1]

All men desire peace, but not all care for those things which make for true peace.

My peace is with the humble and gentle of heart. Your peace will be in much patience.

If you will hear Me and follow My words, you will enjoy much peace.

What then shall I do?

In everything take heed to yourself, what you are doing and what you are saying, and direct your whole attention to please Me alone, not desiring or seeking anything apart from Me.

As for the words or deeds of others, do not judge anything rashly, nor busy yourself with things not committed to your care. If you do this, it may be that you are seldom or little disturbed.

2. But never to feel any disturbance at all, nor to suffer any grief of heart or body does not belong to this present life but to the state of eternal rest.

Do not think, then, that you have found true peace if you feel no heaviness, or that all is well when you have no adversity, or that all is perfect if all things happen as you desire.

Do not think at all highly of yourself, nor account yourself to be especially beloved if you are in a state of great devotion and sweetness, for it is not in such things that a true lover of virtue is known, nor does the true progress and perfection of a man consist in these things.

In what then, Lord?

In giving yourself with all your heart to the divine will; in not seeking your own interest in either great matters or small, in time or in eternity.

In this way you will be able with the same equal countenance to give thanks both in prosperity and adversity, weighing all things in an equal balance.

If you should come to be so valiant and patient in hope that when inward consolation is withdrawn, you can prepare your heart to suffer even more, and yet do not justify yourself as though you should not suffer such great afflictions, but acknowledge My justice in all My appointments, and do not cease to praise My holy name:

Then you are walking in the true and right way of peace, and you may hope without any doubt to see My face again with great joy.

If you arrive at an utter contempt of yourself, know that you shall then enjoy an abundance of peace as great as is possible in the state of your sojourn here.

[1]*John 14:27*

Chapter 26

On Gaining Freedom of Mind Through Humility

Lord, this is the work of a man who would be perfect, never to let his mind slacken from attention to heavenly things and to pass through the many cares as if he had no care—not in sluggish passivity, but with the certainty of a free mind which does not cleave to any created thing or person with inordinate affection.

2. I beseech You, most compassionate God, preserve me from the cares of this life, that I not become too entangled in them; preserve me from the many necessities of the body, that I may not be ensnared by carnal pleasure; from all hindrances of the soul, lest being disheartened, I should be cast down.

I do not speak only of such vanities as the worldly covet with eager desire, but of the miseries which are the common lot of mortal men, miseries which grieve the soul of Your servant and keep him back and make him unable to enter into the freedom of the Spirit whenever he would.

3. O my God, unspeakable sweetness, make bitter to me all fleshly delights which would draw me away from the love of things eternal, and would wickedly allure me to sin by setting before me some present delight.

Let not flesh and blood prevail against me, my God, let them not prevail! Let not the world and its brief glory deceive me! Let not the devil and his devices trip me up!

Give me strength to resist, patience to endure, and constancy to persevere.

Give me, instead of all the consolations of this world, the sweetest unction of Your Spirit, and instead of carnal love, send into my soul the love of Your name.

4. Behold, food, drink, clothing, and other necessities of the body are burdensome to a fervent spirit.

Grant me to use such refreshments with moderation, and not to be entangled with an excessive desire for them.

It is not allowed us to cast them all away, for nature must be sustained. But Your holy law forbids us to seek excess of things for mere pleasure; for then the flesh would grow insolent against the spirit. Between these, let Your hand govern and direct me, I beseech You, that nothing be done in excess.

Chapter 27

On the Evil of Self-Love

Son, it behooves you to give all for all, and to keep nothing of yourself from Me.

Know that self-love hurts you more than anything else in the world.

Things cling to you and hold you to a greater or lesser degree, according to the love you have for them.

If your love is pure, simple, and well ordered, you will be free from bondage to any earthly thing.[1]

Do not sinfully desire anything that is not lawful for you to have, and do not seek to have anything that may hinder you or deprive you of inward liberty.

It is strange that you do not commit yourself fully to me with all your heart, together with everything you may have or desire.

2. Why do you consume yourself with vain grief?[2] Why do you weary yourself with needless cares?

Submit to My good pleasure and you will suffer no loss.

If you seek this or that, and want to be in this place or that, to enjoy your own advantage and good pleasure, you will never be at rest or free from anxiety, for in everything you will find some defect and in every place there will be someone to cross you.

3. It is not, then, obtaining or multiplying outward things that avails, but rather despising and rooting them out of your heart.

This is not to be understood only of money and riches, but also with regard to the quest for honor and the desire for vain praise, which quickly vanish and pass away with the world.

No place suffices if the spirit of fervor is lacking. Any peace which comes from outward things cannot stand long if the true foundation of the heart is lacking. You may change your place, then, but not better yourself.

For when the new occasions arise, you will find in them the same thing from which you fled—yes, and even more!

Prayer for a Pure Heart and for Wisdom

4. Strengthen me, O God, by the grace of the Holy Spirit.[3]

Give me grace to be strong in the inner man[4] and to cast out of my heart all needless care and anxiety,[5] so that I will not be drawn away by vacillating desires for anything whatever, whether it be of great value or little; but teach me to look on all things as passing away and myself as soon to pass away with them.

For nothing is lasting under the sun, where all is vanity and vexation of spirit. O how wise is he who considers it to be so.

5. Give me, O Lord, heavenly wisdom[6] that I may learn to seek and find You above all things, to relish and love You above all things, and to understand all other things as they really are, as ordained in Your wisdom.

Give me grace wisely to avoid him who flatters me, and to bear patiently with him who opposes me; for it is great wisdom not to be carried about by every wind of words,[7] nor to give ear to the false flattery of the siren. Thus shall I go on securely in the way I have begun.

[1]*Matthew 6:22* [2]*Exodus 18:18, Micah 4:9* [3]*Psalm 51:12*
[4]*Ephesians 3:16* [5]*Matthew 6:34* [6]*Ecclesiastes 1:14, 2:1*
[7]*Ephesians 4:14*

CHAPTER 28

On Disregarding Slander

Son, you must not let it grieve you if some think ill of you and say what you would rather not hear.[1]

You ought to think worse things of yourself and believe that no one is weaker than yourself.

If you walk in the Spirit you will care little for such fleeting words.

It is very prudent to be silent in the evil time and to turn within to Me, and not to be disturbed by man's judgment.[2]

2. Do not let your peace depend on what men say, for whether they put a good or bad interpretation on what you do, that does not make you anything other than what you are. You are what you are.

Where are true peace and glory? Are they not in Me?[3]

And he who neither desires to please others nor is afraid to displease them, shall enjoy much peace.

All uneasiness of heart and anxiety of mind arise from inordinate love and vain fear.

[1]*I Corinthians 4:13* [2]*Isaiah 41:11,12* [3]*John 16:33*

Chapter 29

On Seeking God in Tribulation

Blessed be Your name forever, O Lord, for it is Your will that this temptation and tribulation come upon me.

I cannot escape it, but I must of necessity flee to You, that You may help me and turn it to my good.

Lord, I am now in trouble and my heart is not at ease, for I am greatly vexed with this present passion.

And now, beloved Father, what shall I say? I have been brought into a tight place; save me from this hour.[1]

But for this cause I came to this hour, that You might be glorified when I am effectually humbled and delivered by You.

May it please You, O Lord, to deliver me,[2] for poor wretch that I am, what can I do, and whither shall I go without You?

Give me patience, Lord, once again. Help me, my God, and I shall not fear or dread whatever troubles come.

2. And now in the midst of these things, what shall I say?

Lord, Your will be done! I have well deserved to be afflicted and grieved.

I must without doubt bear it, and O that I may bear it with patience until the storms be past and it is better!

But Your almighty hand is able to remove this trial from me and to moderate its violence, so that I may not utterly sink under it, as You have so often done before, my God, my mercy!

And the harder it is for me, so much the easier it is for You. And when I am delivered I can say, "This change was wrought by the right hand of the Most High!"

[1]*John 12:27* [2]*Psalm 40:17*

CHAPTER 30

On Confidence of Grace Restored

Son, I am the Lord, who sends comfort in time of tribulation.[1]

Come to Me when it is not well with you.[2]

What most of all hinders heavenly consolation is that you are too slow in turning yourself to prayer.

For before you pray heartily to Me, you seek many other comforts and refresh yourself in outward things.

Hence, all you do avails you but little until you consider well that I am He who delivers all who trust in Me; and that apart from Me there is no effectual help, no profitable counsel or lasting remedy.

But now, having recovered from your tempest of troubles, take strength again in the light of My mercies. For I am at hand to help you (says the Lord), to restore all things again, not only to their former wholeness, but also much more, in great abundance.

2. Is there anything too hard for Me? Shall I be like one who promises but does not perform?[3]

Where is your faith? Stand firmly and with perseverance. Take courage and be a man of courage! Consolation will come to you in its own time.

Wait for Me! Wait! I will come and heal you.

It is but a temptation, this thing that vexes you, and it is a vain fear that frightens you.

What else does anxiety about the future bring you but sorrow upon sorrow? "Sufficient to the day is the evil of it."[4]

It is a vain and unprofitable thing to be either disturbed or pleased about future things, which perhaps will never happen.

3. But it is the nature of man to be deluded with such imaginations; and it is a sign of a soul as yet weak, to be so easily deceived by the suggestions of the enemy.

For he does not care whether he dupes and deceives you by true things or by false; whether he overthrows you by your love of things present or your dread of things to come.

"Do not let your heart be troubled, neither let it be afraid."[5]

Believe in Me, and put your trust in My mercy.

When you think yourself farthest from Me, I am often nearest to you.

When you think that almost all is lost, then often the greatest gain is close at hand.

All is not lost when something happens against your will.

You must not judge according to your present feeling, nor take any trouble or dwell on it, wherever it may come from, as if all hope of escape were taken away.

4. Do not think yourself forsaken, even though for a time I have sent you some trouble, or have withdrawn your cherished comfort, for this is the way to the kingdom of Heaven.

Without doubt it is better for you and for My other servants that you be proved with adversities, than that you should have everything as you would.

I know your hidden thoughts. I know that it is very expedient for your salvation for you sometimes to be left without spiritual enjoyment, lest you should be puffed up with good success and think yourself better than you are.

What I have given, I can take away, and restore again when I please.

5. When I give it, it is still mine; when I withdraw it, I do not take anything that belongs to you; for every good and every perfect gift is mine.[6]

If I send you trouble or heaviness, fret not, neither let your heart fail you. I can quickly lift you up again and turn all your heaviness into joy.

Nevertheless, I am righteous and greatly to be praised when I deal with you thus.

6. If you are wise and consider this aright, you ought never be so mournful and dejected over any adversity; rather you should rejoice and give thanks.

Yes, you should account this your special joy, that I afflict you with sorrows and do not spare you.

"As my Father has loved me, so have I loved you,"[7] I said to my disciples; yet I sent them out, not to temporal joys, but to great conflicts; not to honors, but to contempt; not to ease, but to toils; not to rest, but to bring forth much fruit with patience. Remember these words well, My son!

[1]*Nahum 1:7* [2]*Matt. 11:28* [3]*Gen. 18:14; Ps. 77:8* [4]*Matt. 6:34*
[5]*John 14:1* [6]*James 1:17* [7]*John 15:9*

Chapter 31

On Leaving the Creature for the Creator

Lord, I am in much need of greater grace if I am to attain that state where neither man nor any creature can hinder me.

For as long as anything holds me back, I cannot flee freely to You.

He desired to flee freely to You who said, "O! that I had wings like a dove! for then I would flee away and be at rest."[1]

What is more at rest than the single eye?[2] And who is

more free than one who desires nothing on this earth?

A man ought to rise above every creature and completely forsake himself as well, to see, in ecstasy of mind, that You, the Creator of all things, have nothing among Your creation that compares with You.

Unless a man is disentangled from all creatures, he cannot freely make divine things his aim.

This is why there are so few contemplatives, because so few know how to separate themselves entirely from perishing and created things.

2. For this a great grace is needed to lift up the soul and bear it above itself.

Unless a man is lifted up in spirit and freed from dependent love of created things and wholly made one with God, whatever he knows, whatever he has is of little account.

He will long remain poor and dejected who esteems anything great save the one infinite eternal good.

Whatever is not God is nothing and ought to be accounted as nothing.

There is a great difference between the wisdom of an enlightened and devout man, and the knowledge of a learned and studious clerk.

Far more worthy is that learning which flows from above, from the divine influence, than that which is laboriously gained by human ingenuity.

3. Many desire contemplation, but they will not practice such things as are required for it.

It is a great impediment that we depend on signs and things of sense and have so little of complete mortification.

I do not know how it is, or by what spirit we are led, or what we intend, we who seem to be called spiritual, that we take such pains and are so full of anxiety about transitory and low things, and so rarely gather our senses fully together to think about our own inner life.

4. Alas! Shortly after a slight recollection, we rush into outward things again, and fail to weigh our works with strict examination.

We do not pay attention to where our affections lie, nor do we bewail the impurity of our motives.

For "all flesh had corrupted their way upon the earth: and for this reason the great Flood came."[3]

When our inward affections are corrupted, it is inevitable that our deeds proceeding out of them will also be corrupted, evidence of our inner spiritual poverty.

For from a pure heart springs the fruit of a good life.[4]

5. We are apt to ask what a man has done, but we do not so carefully consider the motives from which he acts.

We ask if he is strong, rich, handsome, a good writer, a good singer, a good workman; but how poor he is in spirit, how patient and meek, how devout and spiritual, is seldom mentioned.

Nature respects the outward things of a man; grace pays attention to the inward.

Nature is often deluded; but grace has her trust wholly in God, and may not be deceived.

[1]*Psalm 55:6* [2]*Matthew 6:22* [3]*Genesis 6:12* [4]*I Timothy 1:5*

Chapter 32

On Self-Renunciation

Son, you cannot have perfect liberty unless you wholly renounce yourself.

All those who are ruled by self-interest and self-love are chained by their own desires. They are covetous, inquisitive, and unsettled, always seeking their own ease and not the things of Jesus Christ; but often planning and devising things which will not last.

For all that is not of God will come to nothing.

Take this brief and perfect word: *Forsake all and you will find all, forsake carnal desires and you will find great rest.*

Imprint well on your mind what I have said, for when you have put it in practice, you will fully understand.

O Lord, this is not the work of one day, nor is it child's play! Rather, in this short word is included the entire perfection of the Religious.

2. Son, you ought not to turn away from God, nor be cast down quickly when you hear of the way of the perfect. Rather, you should be stirred to higher things, or at least sigh after them with an earnest desire.

Would that you would come to the place where you are no longer moved by self-love, but stood ready at My bidding and at his whom I have given as a father over you. Then you would please Me greatly, and all your life would pass in joy and peace.

You have yet many things to forsake, and unless you forsake them wholly, you cannot attain what you desire.

"I counsel you to buy of me gold tried in the fire, that you may become rich,"[1] that is, heavenly wisdom which despises all lower things.

Set aside worldly wisdom, and do not strive to please others or yourself.

3. I have said that you should exchange the things that are precious and of much worth in the sight of mankind for those which men consider useless and worthless.

True heavenly wisdom is regarded by many to be contemptible and of very little value; not having high thoughts of itself, not seeking to be magnified on earth, it is almost forgotten among men. Many indeed praise it with their lips, but in their lives they are far from it. Yet it is the pearl of great price which is hidden from many.

[1] *Revelation 3:18*

Chapter 33

On Inconstancy of Heart

Son, do not trust your feelings, for whatever they are now, they will quickly change.

As long as you live, you will be subject to such changes,[1] even against your will, so that sometimes you will be merry, at other times sad; now at peace, then troubled; now devout, then without devotion; now diligent, now sluggish; now serious, now light.

One who is wise and well trained in the spirit stands fast through these changes, not paying attention to what he feels in himself, or which way the winds of change blow, but that the whole intent of his soul may keep on to its due and desired end.

By such singleness of mind directed toward Me, a man can continue steadfast and stable in the midst of many changes.

2. The purer (that is, more single) the eye of your intent, the more constant will you be in the different storms through which you pass.[2]

But in many, the eye of a pure intention grows dim, quickly diverted to any pleasurable object it meets.

It is rare to find one who is wholly free from the blemish of self-seeking.

So of old came the people to Bethany to Martha and to Mary–not for the sake of Jesus only, but to see Lazarus.[3]

The eye of the intention, therefore, must be purified, so that it may be single and right, and directed to Me beyond all changing things.

[1]*Job 14:2* [2]*Matthew 6:22* [3]*John 12:9*

Chapter 34

On the Sweetness of God's Love

Behold! My God and my all![1] What more would I have and what greater happiness could I desire?

O sweet and delightful word! But only to him who loves the Word, not the world and the things that are of the world.

"My God and my all!" To him who understands this word, enough is said; and to repeat it again and again is pleasant to one who loves You.

When You are present, everything is delightful. But when You are absent, then everything becomes grievous and irksome.

You give tranquility to the heart, great peace and festal joy.

You cause us to take delight in all things and to praise You in all, nor is anything able to bring lasting pleasure without You. If anything is pleasant and gracious, it is because Your grace is present and it is seasoned with Your wisdom.

2. What would not be pleasant to him who has a true enjoyment of You?

And to him who has no desire for You, what can ever yield delight?

The wise men of the world and those who desire the things of the flesh lack Your wisdom; for in the worldly-wise there is much vanity and emptiness, and in the love of the flesh, death itself.[2]

But they who follow You in despising worldly things and in putting to death the deeds of the flesh, are wise indeed, for they are delivered from vanity to truth, from the flesh to the spirit.

These have a relish for God, and whatever good is found in creatures, they refer it all to the praise of their Maker.

Even so, there is a great difference between the sweetness of the Creator and the creature, of eternity and time, of light made and light unmade.

3. O Light eternal, surpassing all created lights,[3] shed the beams of Your brightness from above to pierce all the inmost parts of my heart!

Purify, gladden, enlighten, and quicken my spirit with its powers, that it may cleave fast to You with an abundance of joy.

O when shall that blessed and desired hour come when You will fill me with Your presence and will be all in all to me?

As long as this is not granted me, my joy will not be full.

Alas! The old man still lives in me; he is not wholly crucified; he is not perfectly dead.[4]

He still lusts mightily against the spirit, and wages

inward wars in me, and will not allow the kingdom of my soul to be at peace.[5]

4. But You who rule the power of the sea, and still the swelling of its waves, arise, and help me!

Scatter the nations that delight in wars against me, and crush them in Your might.

Show Your greatness, I beseech You, and let Your right hand be glorified, for I have no other hope or refuge but You, O Lord my God.

[1]*I Corinthians 15:28* [2]*Romans 8:5* [3]*Psalm 27:1*
[4]*Romans 6:6* [5]*Galatians 5:17*

Chapter 35

On the Certainty of Temptation

Son, you are never secure in this life, but as long as you live you will always need spiritual armor.

You live in the midst of enemies and are assailed on the right hand and on the left.

If you do not defend yourself on every side with the shield of patience, you will not go long without a wound.

Moreover, if you do not fix your heart strongly on Me with a sincere will to endure all things patiently for Me, you will not be able to bear the heat of this warfare, nor attain the palm of the blessed.

You should, therefore, go manfully through everything and use a strong hand against whatever withstands you.

To him who overcomes is manna given; but for the sluggard, there is much misery.

2. If you seek rest in this life, how will you then come to the everlasting rest?

Do not set yourself to have much rest here, but rather seek great patience.

Seek true peace, not on earth, but in Heaven; not in men or any other created things, but in God alone.

For the love of God you ought to undergo all things cheerfully–labors and sorrows, trials, temptation, vexations, anxieties, necessities, infirmities, injuries, detractions, rebukes, humiliations, shame, correction, and contempt.

These are aids to virtue; they are the tests of the young soldier of Christ. These forge the heavenly crown.

I will give you an everlasting reward for a short labor, and infinite glory for your transitory shame.

3. Do you think always to have spiritual consolations at your will?

My saints did not always enjoy such consolations. Rather, they had many afflictions and various temptations, and great discomforts.

But they bore themselves patiently and trusted in God rather than in themselves, knowing that the sufferings of this present time are not worthy to be compared to the future glory.[1]

Would you have at once what many others through many tears and great effort have scarcely obtained?

Wait for the Lord. Behave yourself manfully, and be of good courage. Do not be faithless, but stay in your place and do not turn back. Steadfastly lay down both your body and soul for the glory of God.

I will recompense you abundantly, and I will be with you in every tribulation.

[1]*Romans 8:18*

CHAPTER 36

Against the Vain Judgments of Men

Son, rest your heart firmly on the Lord, and do not fear judgment of men when your conscience bears witness to your dutifulness and innocence.

It is good and blessed to suffer such sayings, and it will not be grievous to a humble heart which trusts more in God than in itself.

Many are given to much talking, and because of this, little trust can be given to what they say.

It is not possible to please all people.

Although Paul endeavored to please all in the Lord, and made himself all things to all men, yet it was a small thing with him that he should be judged by man's judgment.

2. He did as much as he could for the edifying and salvation of others, yet he could not avoid being sometimes judged and despised by others.

Therefore he committed all to God, who knows all things, and defended himself by patience and humility against unjust accusations, and against those who thought and spoke baseless lies.

He did at times speak, however, lest the weak should be hurt and stumble by his silence.

3. Who are you that you should fear a mortal man? Today he is, and tomorrow he is seen no more.

Fear God, and you will not need to dread man.

What harm can the words or injuries of any man do to you? He hurts himself rather than you, and he will not be able to escape the judgment of God, whoever he might be.

Keep God before your eyes and do not contend with argumentative words.

If at the present you seem to be defeated and to suffer shame which you have not deserved, do not complain about it and lessen your reward by impatience.

Rather, lift up your eyes to Me in Heaven. I am able to deliver you from all shame and wrong, and to pay every man according to his works.

Chapter 37

On Obtaining Freedom of Heart

Son, renounce yourself and you will find Me.

Give up choosing your own way and all self-seeking and you will always be the gainer.

Greater grace will be added to you the moment you have given up yourself and have not taken yourself back again.

Lord, how often shall I resign myself, and in what ways shall I forsake myself?

Always and at all times, in small things as well as great. I exclude nothing, but I desire that you be stripped in all things of yourself.

Otherwise, how can you be Mine and I yours, unless you are stripped of all self-will, both inward and outward?

The sooner you effect this, the better it will be for you. The more fully and sincerely you do it, the more will you please Me and the greater will be your gain.

2. There are some who resign themselves, but with certain exceptions. They do not wholly trust in God, and so

they busily try to provide for themselves.

There are some who offer all at first, but afterwards are assailed with temptation, and return to their former ways, and thus make no progress in the path of virtue.

They will not attain to the true liberty of a pure heart nor to the grace of a delightful friendship with Me, unless they renounce themselves entirely and offer themselves as daily sacrifice to Me. Without this there neither is nor can be any fruitful union.

3. I have very often said to you, and I say the same thing again: Forsake yourself, resign yourself, and you will enjoy much inward peace.

Give all for all; seek nothing; ask nothing; abide purely and with firm confidence in Me, and you will possess Me; and you will have such freedom in your heart that darkness will not be able to tread you down.

Let this be your whole aim; let this be your prayer, this your desire: that being stripped of all self-seeking you may naked follow Jesus naked, and, dying to yourself, may live eternally for Me.

Then all vain imaginations, evil fantasies, and superfluous cares will vanish.

Then, too, immoderate fear will leave you and inordinate love will die.

Chapter 38

On the Wise Conduct of Our Affairs

Son, you must endeavor with all diligence in every place, in every action, and in all your outward business to keep yourself inwardly free and master of yourself. Be sure that all these things are under you and that you are not under them.

You must be ruler and master of your own actions, not a servant or a hireling

Rather, you should be as a free man and a true Hebrew, going over into the birthright and freedom of the children of God.

For they stand above present things, and contemplate things eternal.

They look on the passing things with the left eye, and with the right they behold the things of Heaven.

Temporal things cannot attract them to hang on to them, but rather they use temporal things to that goodly service ordained and appointed by God, the great high Creator, who has left nothing in His creation without due order.

2. If you stand steadfast in everything and do not judge what you see and hear by the outward appearance nor with a carnal eye, but enter at once in every circumstance like Moses into the tabernacle to ask counsel of the Lord, you will often hear the divine word and come out instructed in many things present and future.

For Moses always had recourse to the tabernacle for clearing away doubts and answering questions, fleeing to the help of prayer in dangers and against the wickedness of men.

You should in like manner flee to the secret tabernacle of your heart and very earnestly implore divine help.

For we read that the reason Joshua and the children of Israel were deceived by the Gibeonites was that they did not first ask counsel of the Lord, but trusting too easily to fair words, were deluded by their counterfeit piety.

Chapter 39

That We Should Not Be Over-Anxious

Son, always commit your cause to Me, and I will take good care of it in due time.

Wait for My ordering, and you will find it is for your good.

Lord, I do most cheerfully commit all to You, for my own care of it avails but little.

Would that I did not hold on to desires for the future that I might always offer myself wholly to Your good pleasure!

2. Son, a man often struggles mightily for something he desires, and when he obtains it, he begins to feel another way; for man's affections do not long continue directed on the same thing, but rather shift from one thing to another.

It is no small gain, then, to forsake yourself even in the smallest thing.

3. True spiritual growth is in denying oneself. A man who has denied himself is very free and secure.

But the old enemy, who opposes all that is good, never ceases to tempt, but day and night lays deadly snares to see if by any means he may catch the unwary in the dark trap of deceit.

Watch and pray (says the Lord) that you enter not into temptation.

Chapter 40

That Man Has No Good Thing in Which to Glory

Lord, what is man, that You are mindful of him, or the son of man that You visit him?"[1]

What has he done for You that You should grant him Your grace?

Lord, how can I complain if You forsake me? Or what may I righteously say if You do not grant me what I ask?

Surely I may truly think and say this: "Lord, I am nothing; I can do nothing"; I have nothing of myself that is good, but in all things I fall short and always tend to nothingness.

Unless You help me and inwardly instruct and teach me, I will become altogether lukewarm and dissolute.

2. But Lord, You are always the same and endure forever,[2] always good, just, and holy, doing all things well, justly, and in holiness; always disposing everything with wisdom.

But I, always inclined backward rather than forward, never remain the same, for seven times are passed over me.[3]

Yet when it pleases You things quickly become better with me, when You stretch forth Your helping hand. For You can help me alone, without human aid, and can so strengthen me that my heart shall no longer be attracted towards other objects, but turned and rest in You alone.

3. Surely if I could cast off all human comfort, either for the sake of attaining to devotion, or because my needs compel me to seek You, finding no comfort in man, then I might well trust in Your grace to give me new visitations and fresh consolations.

4. Thanks be to You from whom all things come whenever it goes well with me.

But I am vanity and nothing in Your sight, an unstable and weak man. Of what then can I glory? Or for what do I desire to be respected? Is it for this nothingness? This would be vain beyond thought!

In very truth, vainglory is a grievous plague, and the worst of vanities, because it draws us from the true glory, and robs us of all heavenly grace.

For while a man pleases himself, he displeases You; while he yearns for the praise of men, he is deprived of true virtue.

5. But true glory and holy gladness is to glory in You[4] and not in self; to rejoice in Your name, not in our own virtue, and to delight in no creature but for Your sake.

Let Your name be praised, not mine: let Your work be magnified, not mine. Let Your holy name be blessed, but let nothing of man's praises be given to me.[5]

You are my glory; You are the joy of my heart.

In You will I glory and rejoice all the day, but as for myself, I will glory in nothing but my infirmities.[6]

6. Let those who will, seek honor of one another.[7] I will seek that which comes from God alone.

For all human glory, all temporal honor, all worldly grandeur is vanity and folly compared to Your eternal glory.

O Truth! O Mercy! O Blessed Trinity! To You alone be honor, laud, praise, and glory for ever and ever.[8]

[1]*Psalm 8:4* [2]*Psalm 102:12*
[3]*Daniel 4:16* Note: This obscure quotation is found several times in the Book of Daniel, and seems here to refer to Nebuchadnezzar's base character. *(Daniel 4:17)*
[4]*Habakkuk 3:18* [5]*Psalm 113:3, 115:1* [6]*II Corinthians 12:5*
[7]*John 5:44* [8]*I Timothy 1:17*

Chapter 41

On Despising All Temporal Honor

Son, do not be troubled if you see others honored and exalted, and yourself despised and humiliated.

Lift up your heart to Heaven, to Me, and the slights of men will not grieve you.

Lord, we dwell in great darkness and are soon seduced by vanities.

If I inspect myself well, never was any wrong done to me by any creature; and therefore I cannot justly complain to You.

2. Because I have often and grievously sinned against You, all creatures are just when they take arms against me.

Shame and spite, therefore, are due to me, but to You praise, honor, and glory.

Unless I prepare myself so that I would gladly be despised and forsaken by all creatures, and to be esteemed as nothing at all, I cannot obtain inward peace and stability, nor be spiritually enlightened, nor be fully united to You.

Chapter 42

That Our Peace Is Not to Rely on Men

Son, if you set your peace in any person, for your own pleasure in his friendship, you will always be unstable and never content.

But if you always have recourse to the ever-living and abiding Truth, the death or departure of a friend will little grieve you.

Your regard for your friend ought always to be grounded in Me, and he is to be beloved for My sake, whoever he is that you think well of, and who is very dear to you in this life.

Without Me, no friendship is firm or will long endure; nor is that love true and pure that is not held together by Me.

You ought to be so dead to such affections towards your friends, that, inasmuch as is in you, you would consent willingly to be without all human company.

Man approaches as much nearer to God as he departs from all earthly solace.

And the lower he descends in himself, and the meaner and viler he becomes in his own sight, the higher he ascends toward God.

But he who attributes any goodness to himself withstands the grace of God, and hinders its life in him; for the grace of the Holy Spirit ever seeks a humble and meek heart.

If you knew perfectly how to annihilate your self-life, and wholly put out of your heart all human and creaturely love, then I would pour Myself into you with abundant grace.[1]

But when you look to creatures, then the sight of the Creator is rightly hidden from you.

Learn to overcome yourself in all things for the love of the Creator. Then you will be able to attain spiritual knowledge.

No matter how small a thing is, if it is loved inordinately, it holds you back from the highest and corrupts you.

[1]*I Peter 5:5*

Chapter 43

Against Vain and Worldly Learning

Son, do not let the fair and subtle words of men move you. For the kingdom of God is not in word, but in power.[1] Give attention to My words, because they kindle hearts and enlighten minds; they bring compunction and carry with them many a consolation.

Never read the Word in order to appear more learned or wise.

Study rather the mortification of your sins, for this will help you more than the knowledge of many knotty questions.

2. When you have read and learned many things, you must always return to the one principle.

I am He who teaches man knowledge, and I bestow to little ones clearer understanding than can be taught by man.

He to whom I speak will quickly be wise and shall make much progress m spirit.

Woe to them who seek for curious things from men and care little about how to serve Me.

The time will come when Christ, the Teacher of teachers, the Lord of angels, will appear to hear the lessons of all–that is, to examine the consciences of everyone.

Then He will search Jerusalem with candles, and the hidden things of darkness will be brought to light, and all the arguments of men's tongues will be hushed.[2]

3. I am He who in an instant elevates an humble mind, so that a man will understand more of eternal truth than if he had studied ten years in the schools.

I teach without noise of words, without confusion of opinions, without desire for honors, without the wrangling of arguments.

I am He who teaches men to despise earthly things, to be weary of the present, to seek eternal things, to relish things eternal, to flee honors, to endure scandals, to place all hope in Me, to desire nothing out of Me, and to love Me ardently above all things.

4. A certain man, who loved Me with his entire being, became well-taught in spiritual things, and spoke things wonderful.

He profited more by forsaking all things than by studying subtleties.

To some I speak common, plain things; to others, special things. To some I gently show Myself in signs and figures, while to some I reveal mysteries in much light.

A book has but one voice, but it does not instruct everyone alike. For I am the Teacher of truth within, I am the searcher of the heart, the discerner of the thoughts, the mover of actions, distributing to every man as I deem fit.[3]

[1]*I Corinthians 4:20* [2]*Zephaniah 1:12, I Corinthians 4:5* [3]*I Corinthians 12:11*

Chapter 44

On Avoiding Outward Distractions

Son, in many things it is well for you to be ignorant, and to esteem yourself as dead upon earth, as one to whom the whole world is crucified.[1]

You must also pass by many things with a deaf ear, and rather think of those things which belong to your peace.

It is more useful to turn the eye of the soul away from things that displease you and to leave everyone to his own opinion than to be a slave of contentious arguments.

If it is well between you and God, and if you have His judgment in your mind, you will all the more easily endure defeat.

2. Lord, to what are we come? Behold a temporal loss is greatly mourned. For a very small gain men run and toil, while the spiritual loss is soon forgotten, and is hardly ever remembered.

That which avails little or nothing takes up our thoughts, and that which is needed above everything is carelessly passed over. The whole man is taken up with external things, and unless he quickly recovers himself, he becomes content to wallow in them.

[1]*Galatians 6:1*

Chapter 45

On Being Wary of What We Hear

Grant me help, Lord, in tribulation, for vain is the help of man.[1]

How often have I not found faithfulness where I had thought myself sure of it.

And how often, too, have I found it where I least expected it.

It is vain, therefore, to trust in men; the safety of the righteous is in You alone, O God.

Blessed are You, O Lord God, in all things which befall us.

We are weak and unstable, quickly deceived and changed.

2. Who is the man who can so carefully and circumspectly keep himself in all things, as never to fall into some deception or perplexity?

But he who trusts in You, Lord, and seeks You with an undivided heart does not fall so easily.

And if he comes into any tribulation, even though he is much entangled, he will quickly be either delivered or consoled by You. For you will not forsake him who trusts in You, even to the end.

A faithful friend is rarely to be found that continues trustworthy in all the distresses of his friend.

You, Lord, You alone, are most faithful at all times, and there is none like You.

3. How wise was that holy soul who said, "My mind is firmly settled and grounded in Christ."[2]

If it were so with me, I would not be so easily vexed by the fear of man nor would the words of man so easily trouble me.

Who can foresee all things, or guard against all future evils? If things even foreseen nevertheless sometimes hurt us, how can things unlooked for fail to wound us grievously?

But, wretch that I am, why did I not provide better for myself? Why also have I so easily trusted others?

But we are men, nothing else but frail men, even though by many we may be reputed as angels.

In whom shall I put my trust but You, Lord? In whom but You? You are the Truth, who can neither deceive nor be deceived.

On the other hand, "every man is a liar,"[3] weak, unstable, subject to fall, especially in words. So we ought not give instant credence to what seems in appearance to sound right.

4. How wisely You warn us to beware of men,[4] and that a man's foes are those of his own household;[5] and that we should not believe if anyone should say, "Lo, here," or "Lo, there."[6]

My hurt has been my teacher, and would that it might serve to make me more cautious and not more foolish.

"Be wary," says one, "Be wary! Keep what I tell you to yourself." Then, while I hold my peace and think it is a secret, he cannot himself keep the secret he asked me to keep, but presently betrays both himself and me, and goes his way.

From such tales and such indiscreet persons protect me, O Lord! May I neither fall into their hands nor ever commit such things myself.

Put a true and trustworthy word in my mouth, and remove far from me a crafty tongue.

What I am not willing to suffer in others, I ought by all means to avoid myself.

5. How good it is, and how peaceable to be silent about others and not to believe indiscriminately all that is said,

nor to hand on to others reports of what we have heard!

How good it is to open oneself only to a few, and always to be seeking after You, the Searcher of the heart.

We should not be carried about with every wind of words, but we should desire that all things, inward and outward, should be accomplished according to the pleasure of Your will.

How safe it is for retaining heavenly grace, to avoid appearances and not to seek those things which seem to cause admiration from others, but to follow with all zeal and diligence things which bring about amendment of life and zeal.

6. How many there are who have been greatly harmed when their virtue itself was recognized and too hastily praised!

How rich has been the profit of grace guarded by silence in this frail life, which has been called all temptation and warfare.

[1]*Psalm 60:11*
[2]The words are those of St. Agatha, who was martyred during the persecution of Decius, A. D. 251.
[3]*Romans 3:4* [4]*Matthew 10:17*
[5]*Micah 7:6, Matt. 10:36* [6]*Mark 13:21, Luke 17:23*

Chapter 46

On Putting Our Whole Trust in God

Son, stand firm and trust in Me.[1] What are words but words?

They fly through the air, but they do not hurt a rock.

If you are guilty, see to it that you are glad to amend

yourself; if you know nothing against yourself, resolve to suffer this gladly for God's sake.

It is a small matter to suffer at times a few words if you do not yet have courage to suffer hard stripes.

Why do such small things go to your heart, if not because you are still carnal and regard men much more than you should?

Because you are afraid to be despised, you are not willing to be blamed for your faults, but seek the shelter of excuses.

2. But look more carefully into yourself and you will find that the world is yet alive in you, and a vain desire to please men.

When you refuse to be abased and humiliated for your faults, it is evidence that you are neither truly humble nor dead to the world, nor is the world crucified to you.

Give diligence to hear My Word and you will not care for ten thousand words of men.

Think, if all were spoken against you that the worst malice could invent, what hurt could it do you if you would allow it to pass entirely by you and count it no more than a straw? Could it so much as pluck one hair from your head?[2]

3. But he who does not guard his heart inwardly and does not have God before his eyes is easily moved by a sharp word of criticism.

But he who trusts in Me and desires not to stand on his own judgment will be free from the fear of men.

I am the Judge and discerner of all secrets; I know how the thing was done; I know him who offered the injury and the one who suffered it.

This proceeded from Me. This happened with my permission, that the thoughts of many should be revealed.[3]

I shall judge the innocent and the guilty; but by a secret judgment I tried them beforehand.

4. The testimony of men often deceives, but my judgment is true; it will stand and not be overthrown.[4]

It is commonly hidden and not known in all respects, except to a few. Yet it never errs, nor can it err, although to the eyes of the foolish it does not seem just.

Men should therefore appeal to me in every judgment and you must not lean on your own judgment.

For the just man will not be moved, no matter what befalls him from God; and if any wrong charge is brought against him, he will not greatly care.[5]

Yet neither will he rejoice with foolish gladness if he is reasonably excused by others.

He considers that I am He who searches the heart and tries the reins, who judges not according to the exterior nor according to human appearances.[6]

In My sight that is often found worthy of blame which in the judgment of men is thought to be commendable.

Lord God, the just Judge, strong and patient, you know the frailty and perverseness of men. Be my strength and all my trust, for my own conscience does not suffice me.

You know that which I do not know. Therefore in every rebuke I ought to have humbled myself and borne it in meekness.

In Your mercy, therefore, pardon me for those times when I have not done this, and give me once again Your grace for greater endurance.

For Your abundant mercy will better obtain my pardon than any fancied righteousness I might offer for my defense.

Although my conscience does not accuse me, yet I cannot thereby justify myself;[7] for without Your mercy, no man living shall be justified in Your sight.[8]

[1]*Psalm 37:3* [2]*Lk. 21:18, Matt. 10:30* [3]*Luke 2:35* [4]*Psalm 19:9*
[5]*Proverbs 12:21* [6]*Ps. 7:9, I Sam. 16:7* [7]*I Cor. 4:4* [8]*Psalm 143:2*

Chapter 47

On Enduring Hard Things for the Sake of Eternal Life

Son, do not let yourself be dismayed by the labors which you have undertaken for Me, neither let yourself be cast down because of any tribulations which come to you. But let My promise strengthen and comfort you in all events.

I am well able to reward you above all measure and degree.[1]

You will not labor long here, nor always be grieved with sorrows.

Wait a little while and you will see a speedy end to all your troubles.

There will come an hour when all toil and tumult will cease.

Little and brief is all that passes away with time.

2. Do what you have to do with all your might.[2] Labor faithfully in My vineyard.[3] I will be your reward.

Write, read, sing, sigh, keep silence, pray; bear crosses manfully; life everlasting is worthy of all these conflicts and even greater things than they.

Peace will come in a day known to the Lord. It will not be day and night as in this life, but eternal day, with infinite brightness, abiding peace, and unending rest.

Then you will not say, "Who shall deliver me from the body of this death?"[4] Neither will you need to cry, "Woe is me that my sojourning is prolonged!"[5] For death shall then be destroyed, and never-failing health will be without end. There will be no more anxious thoughts, but blessed joy, and sweet and blessed fellowship.

3. O if you had seen the everlasting crowns of the saints in Heaven and in what great glory they now rejoice, who in times past were esteemed by this world as contemptible and judged unworthy even of life itself, truly you would quickly humble yourself to the ground, and would seek rather to be under everyone than to have command over anyone.

You would not long for the pleasant days of this life, but would rather rejoice to suffer tribulation for God, and regard as your greatest gain to be despised and regarded as nothing among the people.

4. O if you had a relishing of these things, and would allow them to sink deeply into your heart, how could you dare to complain even once?

Should not all labors gladly be endured for the joys everlasting?

It is no small matter to lose or gain the kingdom of God.

Lift up your face therefore to Heaven. Behold! I and all My saints with Me, who have had great conflicts in this world now rejoice, are comforted, are now secure, are now at rest. And they shall remain with Me for all eternity in the kingdom of My Father.

[1]*Genesis 15:1* [2]*Ecclesiastes 9:10* [3]*Matthew 20:7*
[4]*Romans 7:24* [5]*Psalm 120:5*

Chapter 48

On Eternity and the Difficulties of This Life

O most blessed home in the city above![1] O cloudless day of eternity, which no night darkens, but which is perpetually lightened by the supreme Truth! O day ever joyful, ever secure and never changing!

O would that day had dawned and that all these things of time had come to an end!

To the saints indeed it shines, resplendent with everlasting brightness; but to those who are pilgrims on the earth, only as far off and through a glass.[2]

2. The citizens of Heaven know how joyful that day is, but the banished children of Eve bewail themselves that this our day is bitterness and sorrow.

The days of this life are short and evil, full of sorrow and anguish.[3]

Here is a man defiled with many sins, ensnared by many passions, held fast by many fears, racked by many cares, distracted by many curiosities, entangled by many vanities, compassed about with many errors, worn down with many labors, burdened with temptations, weakened by pleasures, and tormented by want.

3. O when shall the end come of all these troubles? When shall I be delivered from the miserable bondage of my sins?[4] When shall I be mindful of You alone, Lord?[5] When shall I fully rejoice in You?

When shall I have steady peace, peace undisturbed and secure, peace within and peace without, peace in every way assured?

Good Jesus, when shall I stand to see You? When shall I

contemplate the glory of Your kingdom? When will You be all in all to me?

When shall I be with You in Your kingdom which You have prepared for Your beloved from all eternity?[6]

I am left, a poor and banished man in the land of my enemies, where there are daily wars and great misfortunes.

4. Comfort my exile, assuage my sorrow, for my whole desire sighs after You.

For all is burdensome to me, whatsoever the world offers me for my solace.

I long to enjoy You in my inmost soul, but I cannot lay hold on You.

I desire to cling to heavenly things, but temporal things and unmortified passions weigh me down.

With my mind I desire to be above all these things, but with the flesh I am forced against my will to be subject to them all.

Thus, unhappy man that I am, I fight with myself, and have become a burden to myself, while the spirit seeks to be above and the flesh to be below.

5. O what I suffer inwardly while I dwell in my mind on heavenly things and presently a swarm of carnal thoughts besieges me while I pray. My God, be not far from me; nor turn away in wrath from Your servant.[7]

Cast forth Your lightning and disperse them; shoot out Your arrows and let all the vain fantasies of the enemy be confounded.[8]

Gather in and call home my senses to You; make me forget all worldly things; enable me to cast away speedily and to despise all the imaginations of wickedness.

Help me, O eternal Truth, that no vanity may be my motive.

Come to me, heavenly Sweetness, and let all impurity flee from before Your face.

Pardon me and in Your mercy forgive me, as often as in prayer I think on anything besides You.

I truly confess that I am wont to yield to many distractions.

For often I am not there, where I stand or sit, but rather I am where my thoughts carry me.

Where my thought is, there I am, and often my thought is with what I love.

The thing too readily occurs to me which delights me naturally or which by habit is most pleasing to me.

6. For this reason, You, O Truth, have plainly said, "Where your treasure is, there will your heart be also."[9]

If I love Heaven, I willingly think on heavenly things.

If I love the world, I rejoice in the prosperity of the world and grieve at its adversity.

If I love the flesh, I often picture to myself the things of the flesh.

If I love the Spirit, I delight to think on spiritual things.

For whatever I love, of that I willingly speak and hear, and carry home with me the mental image of it.

But blessed is the man who for Your sake, Lord, gives all created things permission to depart, who does violence to his nature, and through fervor of spirit crucifies the lust of the flesh, so that with a serene conscience he may offer pure prayer to You, and, all earthly things external and internal being shut out, he may be worthy to be among the choirs of angels.

[1]*Revelation 21:2* [2]*I Corinthians 13:12* [3]*Job 7*
[4]*Romans 7:24* [5]*Psalm 71:16* [6]*Matthew 25:34*
[7]*Psalm 71:12, 25:16* [8]*Psalm 144:6* [9]*Matthew 6:21*

Chapter 49

On the Rewards Promised to Those Who Fight Against Sin

Son, when you feel a yearning for everlasting bliss given you from above, and long to depart out of the tabernacle of this body so that you may behold My glory which is without any shadow of turning,[1] open your heart wide[2] and drink in this holy inspiration with all the desire of your soul.

Give fullest thanks to the heavenly Goodness which treats you with such condescension, visiting you mercifully, stirring you up fervently, powerfully lifting you up so that you will not fall down to earthly things by your own weight.

You did not obtain this by your own thought or endeavor, but only by the condescension of heavenly grace and divine favor, so that you may make further progress in virtue, obtain greater humility, and prepare yourself for future conflicts, and so that you may endeavor to cleave to me with the whole affection of your heart, and serve me with a fervent will.

2. Son, the fire often glows, but the flame does not ascend upward without smoke.

So, the desires of some men are ablaze towards heavenly things, but yet they are not free from the temptations of carnal affection.

Therefore they are not acting solely for the honor of God when they make such earnest prayers to Him.

Your desires are often like these, which you have pretended to be so serious and earnest.

For that is not pure and perfect which is tainted with self-love.

3. Do not ask for what is delightful and profitable to you, but for what is acceptable to Me and is for My honor. For if you judge aright, you ought to prefer and follow My will rather than your own desire or anything whatever that is to be desired.

I know your desire and have heard your frequent groanings.

You long now to enjoy the glorious liberty of the sons of God. Now you would delight in the everlasting habitations, your heavenly home, full of joy. But that hour is not yet present. There still remains another time, a time of fightings, labors, and trials.[3]

You desire to be filled with the supreme Good, but you cannot attain it now.

It is I. Wait for Me (says the Lord) until the kingdom of God come.

4. You must still be tried on this earth and proved in many things.

Consolation will sometimes be given you, but the fullness of it shall not be granted.

Take courage, then, and be valiant in doing[4] as well as in suffering things that are repugnant to nature.

You must put on the new man, and be changed into another man.[5]

You must often do what you do not want to do, and leave undone what you would prefer to do.

What others prefer will go ahead, and what you prefer will not succeed.

That which others say will be heard, and what you say be accounted nothing. Others will ask and receive, while you ask without obtaining.

5. Others will be greatly praised, while you remain unnoticed.

To others this office or that shall be committed, but you

will be accounted fit for nothing.

At this, nature will sometimes complain and grumble, and it is no small thing if you bear it all in silence.

In these and many other ways like them, the faithful servant of the Lord is tried as to how far he can deny and break himself in all things.

There is hardly anything in which you have such need to die to yourself as in allowing and seeing that which crosses your will, especially when that is commanded to be done which seems to you either incongruous or of little use.

And because, being under authority, you dare not resist the higher power, it seems hard to you to walk at another's bidding and wholly to give up your own will.

6. But consider, son, the fruit of these labors, how quickly they will end, and their exceeding great reward, and you will not grudge to bear them. Rather you will have the solace to strengthen your patience.

For instead of that little will that you forsake here, you will forever have your will in Heaven, where you shall have all that you can or may desire.

There you will have within your reach all good without fear of losing it.

There your will, always being one with Mine, will not covet any outward or selfish thing.

There none will resist you, no man will complain of you, no man hinder you, nothing stand in your way. All things you desire will be present to replenish your love and fill it to the full.

There I will give you glory for the reproach you endured here, the garment of praise for sorrow,[6] for the lowest place, a kingly throne for all eternity.

There the fruit of obedience will appear, the labor of repentance will rejoice, and humble submission will be gloriously crowned.

7. At present then, bow yourself humbly under it all, and disregard who said this or commanded it.

Let this be your special care, that whether your superior or your inferior or your equal require anything of you—or simply intimate their desire—that you take it all in good part and with a sincere will try to fulfill it.

Let one man seek this, another that; let this man glory in this, the other in that, and be praised a thousand, thousand times. But for your part, let yourself not rejoice in either this or that, but in the contempt of yourself and in My good pleasure and approval alone.

Let this be your constant desire, that whether in life or death, God may always be glorified in you.[7]

[1]*James 1:17* [2]*Psalm 119:32* [3]*Job 7:1*
[4]*Joshua 1:7* [5]*Ephesians 4:24* [6]*Isaiah 61:3*
[7]*Philippians 1:20*

Chapter 50

On Comfort in Desolation

O Lord God, holy Father, You are blessed both now and forevermore, because as You will, so is it done, and what You do is good.

Let Your servant rejoice in You, not in himself nor in anything else. For You alone are the true joy; You my hope and my crown, You my joy and my honor, Lord.

What does Your servant have but what he has received from You,[1] and that without any merit of his own?

Yours are all things, both what You have given and what You have made.

I am poor and in trouble from my youth;[2] and sometimes

my soul is sorrowful even to tears; sometimes it is disturbed within itself because of sufferings that beset it.

2. I long for the joy of peace; I beg again and again for the peace of Your children, who are fed by You in the light of Your consolation.

If You give peace, if You pour into my heart holy joy, the soul of Your servant will be full of melody and devout in Your praise.

But if You withdraw Yourself, as many times You do, he will not be able to run the way of Your commandments,[3] but rather will bow his knees and smite his breast, because it is not with him as it was yesterday and the day before, when Your light shone on his head,[4] and when he was covered under the shadow of Your wings from the temptations which assaulted him.[5]

3. O righteous Father, ever to be praised, the hour is come that Your servant is to be tried.

O beloved Father, it is meet and right that in this hour Your servant should suffer something for Your sake.

Father, ever to be honored, the hour is come which You foresaw from all eternity should come,[6] that for a short time Your servant should outwardly be oppressed, but inwardly should ever live to You.

That he should for a little while be despised and humbled, and should seem to fail in the sight of men, that he should be broken with sufferings and weaknesses, so that he might rise again with You in the dawn of a new light, and be glorified in Heaven.

Holy Father, You have so appointed and it will be so, and all that which You have commanded is accomplished.

4. This is a favor to Your friend, that he should suffer for love of You and be afflicted in the world, however often

and by whomsoever You permit such trials to befall him.

Without Your counsel and providence and without cause, nothing comes to pass on the earth.

It is good for me, Lord, that you have humiliated me, that I may learn Your righteous judgments,[7] and may cast away all haughtiness of heart and all presumption.

It is good for me that shame has covered my face[8] that I may seek consolation from You rather than men.

I have learned also by this to dread Your unsearchable judgments, because You afflict the just together with the wicked, though not without equity and justice.

5. Thanks be to You that You have not spared my sins, but have punished me with bitter stripes, and have sent me sorrows and anguishes within and without.

There is none else under Heaven who can comfort me, but You only, O Lord my God, the heavenly physician of souls. You smite and heal, You bring down to Hell and bring back again.[9]

Your discipline over me and Your rod itself will teach me.[10]

6. Behold, O beloved Father, I am in Your hands. I bow myself under the rod of Your correction.

Smite my back and my neck and make me to bend my crookedness to Your will.

Make me a dutiful and humble disciple of Yours, as You have sometimes done with me, that I may follow Your slightest nudge.

Unto Your correction I commit myself and everything that is mine; it is better to be chastised here than hereafter.

You know all and every thing, and there is nothing in the conscience of man hidden from You.

Before anything is done, You know it, and have no need that anyone should teach You or remind You of those things that are being done on earth.

You know what is expedient for my spiritual progress, and how greatly tribulation serves to scour off the rust of my sins.

Do with me according to Your good pleasure, and do not cast me away because of my sinful life, known to none so clearly and thoroughly as to You.

7. Grant me, Lord, to know what I ought to know, to love what I ought to love, to praise what is most pleasing to You, to esteem highly what is precious to You, to abhor what is filthy and unclean in Your sight.

Do not allow me to judge according to the sight of the eye, nor to make assessment like that of the ignorant. Rather, with a true judgment, let me discern between things visible and spiritual, and above all always to inquire after the good pleasure of Your will.

8. The minds of men are often deceived in their judgments; the lovers of this world are deceived in loving only things visible.

In what way is a man ever better for being esteemed great by man?

The deceitful deceive the deceitful; the vain man, the vain; the blind, the blind; the weak, in magnifying the weak. In truth they rather put a man to shame while they so vainly praise him. For "what every one is in Your eyes, that he is, and no more," says the humble St. Francis.

[1]*I Corinthians 4:7* [2]*Psalm 88:15* [3]*Psalm 119:35*
[4]*Job 29:3* [5]*Psalm 17:8* [6]*John 16:32*
[7]*Psalm 119:71* [8]*Psalm 69:7* [9]*Psalm 18:16*
[10]*Psalm 18:35*

Chapter 51

On the Comfort of Humble Tasks

Son, you cannot always continue in a state of fervent desire of virtue, nor remain in the highest degree of contemplation. Rather, you must sometimes, because of original corruption, come down to lesser things and bear the burden of this corruptible life and its wearisomeness, even against your will.

As long as you bear this mortal body, you will feel some tediousness and heaviness of heart.

As long as you are in the flesh, then, you ought often to bewail the burden of the flesh because you cannot employ yourself unceasingly in spiritual exercises and divine contemplation.

2. At these times, it is expedient for you to undertake humble and devout works, and to refresh yourself in good actions, to await My coming and heavenly visitation with a firm hope, to bear patiently your banishment and the dryness of your mind, till I again visit you and set you free from all anxieties.

For I will make you forget your toils and enjoy inward rest.

I will spread open before you the pleasant fields of the Scriptures, that with an enlarged heart you may begin to run the way of My commandments.[1]

And you will say, "The sufferings of this present time are not worthy to be compared with the glory that shall be revealed in us."[2]

[1] *Psalm 119:32* [2] *Romans 8:18*

CHAPTER 52

On the Comfort of a Contrite Heart

Lord, I am not worthy of Your consolation nor of any spiritual visitation. Therefore You deal justly with me when You leave me poor and desolate.

Though I could shed a sea of tears, I would still not be worthy of Your consolation.

I am not worthy of anything but to be scourged and punished, because I have grievously and often offended You, and have sinned greatly in many ways.

And so, all things considered, I am not worthy even of the least consolation.

But, O good and merciful God, You do not will that Your works should perish, showing the riches of Your goodness upon the vessels of mercy![1] You vouchsafe to comfort Your servant above human measure and beyond all his deserts.

For Your consolations are not like the chitchat of men.

2. What have I done, Lord, that You should bestow any heavenly comfort upon me?

I do not recall that I have done any good, but rather that I have always been prone to vice and slow to amend.

This is the truth and I cannot deny it. If I should say otherwise, You would stand against me, and there would be no one to defend me.

What have I deserved for my sins but Hell and everlasting fire?

I confess in very truth that I am worthy of all scorn and contempt, and that it is not fit that I should be named among Your devout servants.

And although I do not like to hear this, yet for truth's

sake I will lay bare my sins against myself, so that I may more easily be fit to implore Your mercy.

3. What shall I say, since I am guilty and full of all disorder?

My mouth can utter nothing but this word: "I have sinned, Lord! I have sinned! Have mercy on me and pardon me."

Spare me for a little time, in order that I may lament my sorrow before I go into the land of darkness, a land covered with the shadow of death.[2]

What do You so much require of a guilty and miserable sinner as that he feel contrition and that he humble himself for his sins?

Out of true contrition and the humbling of the heart is born the hope of forgiveness; the troubled conscience is reconciled; grace which was lost is recovered; a man is preserved from the wrath to come, and God and the repentant soul meet together with a holy kiss.

4. Humble contrition for sins is an acceptable sacrifice to You,[3] Lord, a far sweeter odor in Your presence than the smoke of incense.

It is also that pleasing ointment which You would have poured on Your sacred feet:[4] for a contrite and humbled heart You have never despised.[5]

Here is the place of refuge from the angry face of the enemy. Here is effaced and washed away whatever stain has been contracted anywhere.

[1]*Romans 9:23* [2]*Job 10:21* [3]*Psalm 51:17*
[4]*Luke 7:46* [5]*Psalm 51:17*

Chapter 53

On Deadness to Earthly Affections

Son, My grace is precious, and does not allow itself to be mingled with outward things or with worldly consolations.

You must, therefore, cast away every obstacle to grace if you desire to be ready to receive the inpouring of it.

Choose a secret place for yourself. Love to live alone with yourself; do not seek the conversation of anyone. Rather, pour out your devout prayer to God that you may keep your mind contrite and your conscience pure.

Esteem the whole world as nothing; prefer the service of God before all other things.

For you will not be able to serve Me and at the same time delight yourself in transitory pleasures.

You should remove yourself from your acquaintances and friends,[1] and not rely on any worldly comfort.

So the blessed apostle Peter beseeches, that the faithful of Christ would keep themselves as strangers and pilgrims in this world.[2]

2. What great confidence will he have at the hour of death who is not detained by an affection for any passing or transitory thing in the world!

But the unspiritual mind cannot as yet understand what it means to have a heart so freed from all things, nor does the carnal man recognize the liberty of the interior man.[3]

But if a man desires to be truly spiritual, he must give up those who are near him as well as those who are far off, and to beware of none more than of himself.

If you overcome yourself perfectly, you will very easily bring everything else under the yoke.

The perfect victory is to triumph over self.

For he who keeps himself in such subjection, so that his emotions are subject to reason, and his reason is obedient to Me in all things, is indeed a conqueror of himself and lord of the world.

3. If you desire to climb to this height, you must set out bravely and lay the axe to the root,[4] so that you may pull up and destroy that hidden inordinate inclination to self and to selfish and earthly goods.

From this vice, this inordinate love of self, springs almost all that must be utterly rooted out, and once this evil is vanquished and subdued, great peace and tranquility will follow very soon.

But because few labor to die perfectly to themselves or to overcome themselves completely, they remain entangled and cannot be lifted in spirit above themselves.

But he who desires to walk freely with Me, must put to death all his evil and inordinate affections, and must not cling to any created thing with the longing of selfish love.

[1]*Matthew 19:29* [2]*I Peter 2:11* [3]*I Corinthians 2:14* [4]*Matthew 3:10*

Chapter 54

On the Difference Between Nature and Grace

Son, note carefully the movements of nature and grace, for they work in completely opposite yet subtle ways, and can scarcely be distinguished except by one who is spiritually and inwardly enlightened.

All men indeed desire that which is good, and pretend to some good in their words and deeds. Under the show of good, therefore, many are deceived.

Nature is crafty and seduces many, ensnaring and deceiving them, and always has itself for its goal and object.

But grace walks in simplicity, she declines all appearance of evil, she does not shelter herself with deceits, but does all things purely for God, in whom she finally rests.

2. Nature is unwilling to die, or be restrained, or be overcome, nor to be brought into subjection, nor will she of her own accord subject herself.

But grace studiously mortifies herself, resists sensuality, seeks to be in subjection, desires to be kept under, and is not bent on using her own freedom. She loves to be kept under discipline and does not desire to rule over anyone, but always to live, abide, and be under God, and for God's sake is always ready to bow down meekly under human beings.[1]

Nature strives for her own advantage, and considers how to win at another's expense.

Grace does not consider what is profitable and of advantage to herself, but rather what may be for the good of many.[2]

Nature eagerly receives honor and respect.

Grace faithfully attributes all honor and glory to God.[3]

3. Nature fears shame and contempt.

Grace rejoices to suffer reproach for the name of Jesus.[4]

Nature loves leisure and bodily rest.

Grace cannot be idle, and cheerfully seeks some useful labor.[5]

Nature seeks to have things that are curious and beautiful and abhors those that are cheap and coarse.

Grace delights in what is plain and humble, does not disdain rough things, and does not refuse to be clad in old clothes.

Nature respects temporal things, rejoices at earthly gain,

sorrows for losses, and is irritated by every slight, injurious word.

Grace looks intently on things eternal, does not cleave to temporal things, is not disturbed at losses nor exasperated with hard words, because she has placed her treasure and joy in Heaven, where nothing is lost.[6]

4. Nature is covetous, receives more readily than gives, and loves to have personal and private possessions.

Grace is kind-hearted, ready to share with others, and shuns selfish interests. She is content with a little and judges that it is more blessed to give than to receive.[7]

Nature inclines a man to love created things, to his own flesh, to vanities, and to travelling about to see new things.

Grace draws a man to God and to virtue, refusing to follow after created things; she flies from the world, hates the desires of the flesh, and restrains wanderings abroad, and avoids being in the limelight as much as possible.

Nature is glad to have outward comforts by which she may delight her feelings.

Grace seeks consolation in God alone, and delights herself in His sovereign goodness above all visible things.

5. Nature acts solely for her own gain and profit. She does nothing without a price, but for every kindness she hopes to get back something equal or better—or at least praise or favor for her kindnesses. She is very earnest that her works and gifts be highly valued.

Grace seeks nothing temporal, requires no other reward but God alone, and asks for no more temporal necessities than those which may serve in obtaining things eternal.

6. Nature rejoices in a multitude of friends and kinsfolk; she boasts of noble lineage and descent; she fawns on the powerful, flatters the rich, and applauds those who are like herself.

Grace loves even her enemies, is not puffed up with troops of friends, and sets no store by family or lineage unless it is joined with greater virtue.

Grace favors the poor rather than the rich, sympathizes more with the innocent than with the powerful, rejoices with the honest and not with the deceitful.

She ever exhorts the good to strive for the better gifts,[8] and by every virtue to become like the Son of God.[9]

Nature quickly complains of want and of inconvenience.

Grace endures poverty with firmness and constancy.

7. Nature refers everything to herself, argues for herself, strives and fights for herself.

Grace returns all things to God, from which they originally proceed. She ascribes no good to herself, nor does she arrogantly presume. She does not contend nor prefer her own opinion to others; she submits her own understanding and intellect to the eternal wisdom and the divine judgment.

Nature is eager to know secrets and to hear news; she loves to appear in public and to prove many things by her own senses. She loves to be noticed and to do things for which she may be praised and admired.

Grace does not care to hear new and curious matters, because all this rises out of the old corruption of man, and she knows that there is nothing new, nothing durable on the earth. Grace teaches, therefore, to restrain the senses, to shun vain complacency and ostentation, and to hide humbly those things that are worthy of admiration and praise, to seek useful fruit from everything and in all knowledge to the praise and honor of God.

She will not have herself or that which pertains to her extolled, but desires that God should be blessed in His gifts, who bestows all things solely out of His love.

8. This grace is a supernatural light, a certain, special gift of God, the proper mark of the elect, a pledge of eternal salvation. It raises up a man from earthly things to love heavenly things, and from being carnal, makes him a spiritual man.

The more, therefore, nature is denied and subdued, the greater is the grace that is infused, and every day by new visitations, the inward man is renewed in the image of God.[10]

[1]*I Peter 2:13* [2]*I Corinthians 10:33* [3]*Psalm 29:2*
[4]*Acts 5:41* [5]*I Corinthians 15:10* [6]*Matthew 6:20*
[7]*Acts 20:35* [8]*I Corinthians 14:1* [9]*II Peter 1:5*
[10]*Colossians 3:10*

Chapter 55

On the Victory of Grace Over Nature

O Lord my God, who created me after Your own image and likeness, grant me this grace which You have showed me to be so great and necessary to salvation: that I may overcome my very evil nature, ever drawn to sin and perdition.

For I feel in my flesh the law of sin contradicting the law of my mind, and leading me captive to obey sensuality in many things; nor can I resist the passions of it unless Your grace assists me in it.[1]

2. I need Your grace and great grace to overcome nature, which is ever prone to evil from its youth.[2]

For through Adam the first man, nature is fallen and corrupted by sin, and the penalty of this stain has descended on all mankind in such a way that nature itself, which was created good and upright, now stands for corruption and the weakness of man's corrupt nature, because, left to itself, nature ever draws to evil and to base things.

For the small power which remains is, as it were, a spark lying hidden in the ashes.

This is our natural reason itself, encased about with great darkness, yet still retaining power to discern the difference between good and evil, true and false, although it is unable to fulfill all that it approves, and no longer enjoys the full light of truth nor wholeness in its affections.

3. Hence it is, O my God, that I delight in Your law after the inward man, knowing that Your commandment is good, just, and holy, and reproving all evil and sin as things to be avoided.[3]

But with the flesh I serve the law of sin,[4] in that I obey my senses rather than my reason.

Hence it is, that to will what is good is present with me, but I am not able to perform it.[5]

Hence I often purpose many good things, but because I lack grace to help my weakness, even a slight resistance causes me to fall back and fail.

Hence it happens that I know the way of perfection and see clearly enough what I ought to do, but, being pressed down with the weight of my own corruptions, I do not rise to the life that is more perfect.

4. O Lord, how utterly necessary is your grace for me to begin that which is good, to go on with it, and to accomplish it.

Without that grace I can do nothing, but in You I can do all things, when Your grace strengthens me.[6]

O true and heavenly grace! without which our most worthy actions are nothing, and no gifts of nature are of any value!

No arts, no riches, no beauty or strength, no wit or eloquence are of any value before You, without Your grace, O Lord.

Gifts of nature are given to good and bad, but grace or divine love is the peculiar gift of the elect; and they who bear this honorable mark are deemed worthy of eternal life.

So excellent is this grace that neither the gift of prophecy, the working of miracles, nor any speculation, however sublime is of any value without it.

No, not even faith, hope or any other virtues are acceptable to You without divine love and grace.

5. O most blessed grace, which makes the poor in spirit rich in virtues, and renders him who is rich in many goods humble in heart:

Descend upon me! Come and replenish me early with your consolations, lest my soul faint with weariness and dryness of mind.

I beseech You, O Lord, that I may find grace in Your sight, for Your grace is sufficient for me,[7] even though I may obtain none of those things that nature desires.

Although I am tempted and troubled with many trials, yet I will fear no evil so long as Your grace is with me.[8]

Your grace alone is my strength; it gives counsel and help.

Grace is stronger than all my enemies and wiser than all the wise.

6. Your grace is the schoolmistress of truth, the teacher of discipline, the light of the heart, the solace in affliction, the banisher of sorrow, the expeller of fear, the nurse of devotion, the producer of tears.

Without grace, what am I but a withered branch, an unprofitable stock only fit to be cast away?

Let Your grace therefore, O Lord, always precede and

follow me, and make me to be continually intent on good works, through Your Son, Jesus Christ. Amen.

[1]*Romans 7:23* [2]*Genesis 8:21* [3]*Romans 7:22*
[4]*Romans 7:25* [5]*Romans 7:18* [6]*Philippians 4:13*
[7]*II Corinthians 12:9* [8]*Psalm 23:4*

Chapter 56

On Christ, the Way, the Truth, and the Life

Son, the more you can forsake yourself, the more you will be able to enter into Me.

In the same way that peace within comes from desiring nothing outward, so the forsaking of self inwardly unites you to God.

It is My will that you learn perfect renunciation of yourself to My will without resistance or complaint.

Follow Me. I am the way, the truth, and the life.[1] Without the way, there is no going; without the truth, there is no knowing; without the life, there is no living. I am the way, which you must follow; the truth, which you must trust; the life, for which you must hope.

I am the way inviolable, the truth infallible, the life imperishable.

I am the straight way, the supreme truth, the truest life, the blessed life, the uncreated life.

If you abide in My way, you shall know the truth, and the truth shall make you free,[2] and you shall lay hold on eternal life.[3]

2. If you would enter into life, keep the commandments.[4] If you would know the truth, believe Me.[5]

If you would be perfect, sell all.[6]

If you would be My disciple, deny yourself.[7]

If you would possess the blessed life, despise the present life.

If you would be exalted in Heaven, humble yourself in this world.

If you would reign with Me, bear the Cross with Me.

Only the true servants of the Cross can find the way of bliss and true light.

3. O Lord Jesus, since Your way is narrow and despised by the world, grant me grace to follow You even though the world despise me.

For the servant is not greater than his Lord, nor the disciple above his Master.[8]

Let Your servant be trained in Your life, for in it consists my salvation and my true holiness.

Whatever I read or hear besides this does not give me full refreshment or delight.

4. Son, since you know and have read all these things, you will be blessed if you do them.[9]

He who has My commandments and keeps them, he it is who loves Me, and I will love him, and will manifest Myself to him,[10] and will make him sit together with Me in My Father's kingdom.[11]

O Lord Jesus, as You have spoken and promised, so let it come to pass; and grant that it may be my lot to merit it.

I have received the Cross from Your hand; I will bear it, and will bear it even to death, as You have laid it on me.

Truly the life of a good monastic is a Cross, but it leads him to paradise.

We have begun. We may not go back; neither should we abandon it.

5. Courage, then, brothers! Let us go forward together! Jesus will be with us.

For the sake of Jesus we took up this Cross: for the sake of Jesus let us persevere in the Cross.

He will be our helper, who is our captain and forerunner.

Behold, our King goes on before us, and He will fight for us.

Let us follow like men; let no man fear the terrors or the fight! Let us be ready to die in battle, and let us not stain our glory by fleeing from the Cross.

[1]*John 14:6* [2]*John 8:32* [3]*John 8:12*
[4]*Matthew 19:17* [5]*John 14:17* [6]*Matthew 19:21*
[7]*Matthew 16:24* [8]*Matthew 10:24* [9]*John 13:17*
[10]*John 14:21* [11]*Revelation 3:21*

Chapter 57

On Calmness Under Trials

Son, patience and humility in adversity are more pleasing to Me than much consolation and devotion in prosperity.

Why are you so disturbed at every little thing spoken against you?

If it had been much more, you should not have been moved.

But now, let it pass. It is not the first time, nor is it anything new, nor will it be the last, if you live long.

You are courageous enough as long as no adversity or opposition comes in your way.

You can give good advice also, and can encourage others with your words, but when any unexpected trouble comes to your door, you fail in counsel and in courage.

Observe then your great weakness, which you have often experienced in small difficulties.

Yet these things happen to you for your good, regardless of how it seems.

2. Dispel it from your heart as well as you can, and if it has affected you, do not let it cast you down or keep you entangled in it for long.

At the least, bear it patiently even if you cannot bear it joyfully.

Although you are loathe to bear it and are indignant at it, restrain yourself and allow no ill-advised word to pass from your mouth, which may cause Christ's little ones to stumble.

The storm which is now raised shall be quickly abated, and your inward pain will be sweetened by the return of grace.

As I live (says the Lord) I am ready to help you and to give you greater comfort than before if you put your trust in Me and call faithfully on Me.[1]

3. Be more calm of heart and gird yourself for greater endurance.

All is not lost, even if you feel yourself very often afflicted or grievously tempted.

You are man and not God. You are flesh, not an angel.

How can you expect to remain always in the same state of strength, when an angel in Heaven fell, as well as the first man in paradise?

I am He who raises up and saves those who mourn, and those who know their own weakness I advance onward toward My own divine glory.

4. O Lord, blessed be Your word, more sweet to my mouth than honey and the honeycomb.[2]

What should I do in these great tribulations and straits, if You did not encourage me with Your holy words?

What matter is it, how much or what I suffer, if only I

may at length come to the haven of salvation?

Grant me a good end; grant me a happy passage out of this world.

Be ever mindful of me, O my God, and direct me by a straight way to Your kingdom. Amen.

[1]*Isaiah 49:18* [2]*Psalm 19:10, 119:103*

Chapter 58

On the Vanity of Searching into the Secrets of God

Son, be careful not to dispute about high things, nor about the secret judgments of God–why this man is so abandoned, and that man is raised to such great favor; why one man is so greatly afflicted, and another so greatly advanced.

These things are beyond the reach of man, nor is it in the power of any reason or disputation to search out the judgments of God.

When the enemy suggests these things to you, or some curious people raise the question, let your answer be that of the prophet, "You are just, O Lord, and Your judgment is right."[1]

And again, "The judgments of the Lord are true and righteous altogether."[2]

My judgments are to be feared, not to be searched out. They are such as cannot be comprehended by the understanding of man.[3]

2. Moreover, do not inquire or dispute the merits of the saints, which of them is more holy than the other, or which

shall be the greater in the kingdom of heaven.

These things often breed strife and unprofitable contentions. They nourish pride and vainglory, from whence spring envy and disagreement, while one will proudly seek to exalt this one, and another man the other.

To desire to know and search out such things serves no good end, and is painful to the saints, for I am not the God of dissension, but of peace. This peace consists rather in true humility than in self-exaltation.

3. Some are carried with a zeal of love towards these saints or those with greater affection, but this is human love rather than divine.

Am I not He who made all the saints? Moreover, I gave them grace and bestowed glory on them.

I know what every one has deserved, and I have gone before them with the sweetness of my blessing.

I foreknew My beloved ones.

I chose them out of the world; they did not first choose Me.

I called them by grace, I drew them to Me by mercy, I led them through many temptations.

I poured glorious consolations into their hearts. I gave them perseverance, and I have crowned their patience.

4. I know the first and the last, and I embrace all with love inestimable.

I am to be praised in all My saints. I am to be blessed above all things, and to be honored in every one of them whom I have thus gloriously magnified and predestined without any foregoing merits of their own.

Whoever despises one of the least of My saints, therefore, does not honor the greatest, for I made both small and great.

And he who depreciates any of My saints, depreciates Me also, and all the rest who are in the kingdom of Heaven.

They are all one through the bond of love. Their thought is one, their will is one, and they all love each other as one.

5. Still (which is a far higher thing) they love Me more than themselves or any merits of their own.

Being lifted above self, they are wholly freed from love of self and are entirely set on loving Me, in whom they also rest with fullness of joy.

Nothing can turn them back from Me, nothing can thrust them down from their glory, for being full of the eternal truth, they burn with the fire of an unquenchable charity.

Therefore let carnal and natural men who can love nothing but their own delights, restrain themselves from disputing about the state of the saints. Such men add and take away according to their own fancies, not according to what pleases eternal truth.

6. Many are ignorant, especially those, who being but little enlightened, can seldom love anyone with a perfect spiritual love.

They are as yet much controlled by a natural love and human friendship to this man or that, and they imagine that heavenly things will correspond to their experiences of earthly loves.

[1]*Psalm 119:137* [2]*Psalm 19:9* [3]*II Timothy 2:23*

CHAPTER 59

On Placing All Our Hope and Trust in God Alone

Lord, what is my confidence in this life, or what is the greatest comfort I can derive from anything in Heaven?

Is it not you, O Lord my God, whose mercies are without number?

Where has it ever been well with me without You, or when could it be ill with me when You were present?

I had rather be poor for Your sake than rich without You.

I had rather choose to be a pilgrim on earth with You than to possess Heaven without You. Where You are, Heaven is there; and where You are absent, there is death and Hell.

You are all my desire; therefore I must sigh for You, call out to You, and earnestly pray to You.

There is none whom I can fully trust, none that can give me ready help in my necessities but You alone, O my God.

You are my hope; You are my confidence; You are my comforter, in all things most faithful to me.

2. *All men seek their own.*[1] But You, O Lord, seek only to further my salvation and progress in spiritual growth, and turn every thing to my good.

Although You expose me to various temptations and adversities, yet You order all this to my advantage, for You thus try those whom You love in a thousand ways.

In these trials of me, You should be loved no less and praised no less than when You filled me full of heavenly consolations.

3. In You, therefore, O Lord God, I place my whole hope and refuge; on You I rest in my tribulations and anguish, for I find all is weak and unstable, no matter what it is, unless it is in You.

For many friends cannot profit me, nor can strong helpers assist, nor wise counselors give profitable answers, nor can the books of the learned yield any comfort, and no precious substance can deliver, nor can any place, however remote and lovely, give shelter, unless You Yourself assist, help, strengthen, console, instruct, and guard me.

4. Without You, everything that seems to belong to the attainment of peace and happiness is nothing and in truth brings no happiness at all.

You alone are the end of all that is good, the height of life, the depth of wisdom, and to trust in You alone above all things is the strongest comfort to Your servants.

To You, therefore, I lift up my eyes; in You, my God, the Father of mercies, I put my trust.

Bless and sanctify my soul with Your heavenly blessings, that it may become Your holy dwelling place, the seat of Your eternal glory. And let nothing be found in this temple of Your glory to offend the eyes of Your majesty.

According to the greatness of Your goodness and the multitude of Your mercies, look upon me and hear the prayer of Your poor servant, who is exiled far from You in the land of the shadow of death.

Protect and keep my soul, the least of Your servants, amid the many dangers of this corruptible life, and, accompanied with Your grace, direct me along the way of peace to the land of everlasting light. *Amen.*

[1]*Philippians 2:21*

The Fourth Book

Concerning the Sacrament

An Exhortation to Holy Communion

The Voice of Christ

Come to Me, all who labor and are heavy laden, and I will give you rest. *(Matthew 11:28)*

The bread which I shall give for the life of the world is My flesh. *(John 6:51)*

Take, eat: This is My body which is broken for you. Do this in remembrance of Me. *(Luke 22:19, I Corinthians 11:24)*

He who eats My flesh and drinks My blood abides in Me, and I in him. *(John 6:56)*

The words that I have spoken to you are spirit and life. *(John 6:63)*

Chapter 1

On Receiving the Sacrament with Great Reverence

The Voice of the Disciple

These are Your words, O Christ, Eternal Truth, though not spoken at one time, nor written in one place.

Because they are Your words and true, they are all to be received by me with gratitude and faith.

They are Yours, and You have spoken them, and they are mine, too, because You spoke them for my salvation.

I cheerfully receive them from Your mouth, that they may be all the more deeply implanted in my heart.

They stir me, those most gracious words, so full of tenderness and love. But my own sins terrify me, and my impure conscience makes me hesitate to approach so great a mystery.

The sweetness of Your words invites me, but the multitude of my sins weighs heavily on me.

2. You command me to come confidently to You if I would have part in You, and to receive the food of immortality if I desire to obtain everlasting life and glory.

"Come to Me," You say, "all who labor and are heavy laden, and I will refresh you."

O sweet and loving word in the ear of a sinner, that You, my Lord God, should invite the poor and needy to the Communion of Your most sacred Body.

But who am I, Lord, that I should *presume* to come to You?

Lo, the Heaven of heavens cannot contain You, and You say, "Come to Me, all of you"?

3. What does this gracious condescension and this so loving an invitation mean?

How shall I come to You, knowing that I have done nothing well?

How shall I bring You into my house, I who have so often offended Your most gracious countenance?

Angels and archangels stand in awe of You. Holy and righteous men fear You, and yet You say, "Come, all of you to Me"?

If it had not been You, O Lord, who said this, who would believe it to be true?

And if You did not command it, who would dare draw near?

Behold, Noah, a just man, labored a hundred years in the making of the ark, so that he might be saved with a few others. How, then, can I in one hour prepare myself to receive the Maker of the world with due reverence?

4. Moses, Your great servant and special friend, made an ark of incorruptible wood which he covered with pure gold, in which to house the tablets of the Law. How shall I, a foul, corrupted creature, dare so lightly to receive the Maker of the Law and the Giver of life?

Solomon, the wisest of the kings of Israel, devoted seven years to the building of a magnificent temple to the praise of Your name.

He celebrated the dedication of it for eight days on end, and offered a thousand peace-offerings, solemnly setting the Ark of the Covenant in the place prepared for it with the sound of trumpets and shoutings.

And I, the most miserable and poorest of men, how shall I bring You into my house, I who can scarcely spend one half hour in true devotion? And would that I could even once spend something like half an hour in a worthy and fit way!

5. O my God, how earnestly did they endeavor to please You!

Alas, how little it is that I do! How little time I take when I dispose myself to receive Holy Communion!

I am seldom wholly collected; very seldom indeed am I free of all distraction.

Yet surely in this life-giving presence of Your Deity, no unbecoming thought should intrude itself, nor should any creature occupy my mind, for it is not an angel but the Lord of angels whom I am about to entertain.

6. Yet very great is the difference between the Ark of the Covenant with its relics and Your most pure Body with its unspeakable virtues, between the sacrifices of the Law, figures of things to come, and the true sacrifice of Your Body, the fulfillment of all ancient sacrifices.

Why, then, am I not more ardent and zealous in seeking Your Presence?

Why do I not prepare myself with greater care to receive Your sacred gifts, when those holy patriarchs and prophets of old, yes, and kings, too, and princes, with the whole people, showed such great devotion to Your divine worship?

7. The most devout king, David, danced before the Ark of God with all his might, calling to mind the benefits bestowed in time past on the fathers. He made musical instruments of various kinds, he set forth psalms and appointed them to be sung with joy; he also often sang them himself, to the harp, being inspired with the grace of the Holy Spirit. He taught the people of Israel to praise God with their whole heart, and with voices full of harmony to bless and praise Him every day.

If such great devotion was then shown, and such celebration of divine praise was kept up before the Ark of the Covenant, what reverence and devotion should I and all

Christian people have during the celebration of this Sacrament, in receiving the most precious Body of Christ?

8. Many run to various places to visit the relics of departed saints, and are full of wonder at hearing their deeds. They look with awe on the spacious church buildings; they look at and kiss their sacred bones, covered with silk and gold.

And lo, You, my Lord God, You are present here to me on the altar, Holy of holies, Creator of men, and Lord of angels.

Often in seeking such things, men are moved by curiosity and by the novelty of fresh sights, and little or no fruit of amendment is carried home, especially when they go so lightly from place to place without true contrition.

But here, in the Sacrament of the altar, You are wholly present, my God, the man Christ Jesus: here, to all worthy and devout receivers, is granted the abundant fruit of eternal salvation.

There is here nothing to attract men that savors of levity, curiosity, or sense: nothing but firm faith, devout hope, and sincere love.

9. O God, the invisible Creator of the world,[1] how wonderfully You deal with us! How sweetly and graciously You dispose all things concerning Your elect, to whom You offer Yourself to be received in this Sacrament!

Truly this passes all understanding. This specially attracts the hearts of the devout, and enkindles their love.

For Your truly faithful, who dispose their whole life towards amendment often receive a great grace of devotion and love of virtue from this most precious Sacrament.

10. O marvelous and hidden grace of this Sacrament, which only the faithful of Christ know, but which the unbe-

lieving and those who are slaves to sin cannot experience.

In this Sacrament, spiritual grace is given, and virtue which was lost is restored in the soul, and the beauty which had been disfigured by sin returns again.

This grace is sometimes so great that from the abundance of devotion given in it, not only the mind but the weak body also feels a great increase of strength bestowed on it.

11. Nevertheless our coldness and negligence is greatly to be bewailed and deplored, that we are not drawn with greater affection to receive Christ, in whom consists all the hope and merit of those who are to be saved.

For He Himself is our sanctification and redemption.[2] He Himself is the consolation of pilgrims and the everlasting fulfillment of saints.

It is much to be lamented that many take so lightly this saving mystery, which gladdens Heaven and preserves the world.

Alas for the blindness and hardness of the human heart, which does not weigh more deeply so unspeakable a gift, and by the daily habit comes to regard it as little or nothing!

12. If this holy Sacrament were to be celebrated in one place only, and consecrated by only one priest in the world, with what great desire do you think men would be drawn to that place and to such a priest of God, that they might be witnesses of the celebration of these divine mysteries?

But now, many are made priests, and in many places Christ is offered, so that the grace and love of God to man may appear so much the greater, the more widely this Holy Communion is spread over all the world.

Thanks be to You, O good Jesus, Shepherd Eternal,[3] that You have vouchsafed to feed us poor exiles with Your precious Body and Blood, and that You invite us to receive these mysteries with the words even from Your own mouth, saying, "Come unto Me, all who labor and are heavy laden, and I will refresh you."

[1]*Hebrews 11:3* [2]*I Corinthians 1:30* [3]*Hebrews 13:20*

CHAPTER 2

On God's Love in the Eucharist

The Voice of the Disciple

Trusting in Your goodness and great mercy, Lord, I draw near; sick I come to the Savior; hungry and thirsty to the Fountain of life; needy to the King of Heaven, a servant to his Lord, a creature to the Creator, a desolate soul to my merciful Comforter.

But how is it that You come to me?[1] Who am I that You should give Your own self to me?

How dare a sinner appear before You? And how is it that You vouchsafe to come to so sinful a creature?

You know Your servant, You know that he has in him no good thing for which You should grant him this favor.

I confess my unworthiness. I acknowledge Your bounty. I praise Your mercy, and give You thanks for Your great charity.

For You do this of Your own mercy, not for any merits of mine, in order that Your goodness may be better known to me, Your love more abundantly poured down, and humility more perfectly commended to me.

Since it is Your pleasure and You have commanded that it should be so, Your gracious condescension pleases me also, and would that my iniquity might be no hindrance!

2. O most sweet and most merciful Jesus, how great reverence and thanksgiving and perpetual praise are due to You as we receive Your most sacred Body, whose dignity no man is able to express!

What shall my thoughts dwell on at this Communion, in approaching my Lord whom I am never able duly to honor, yet whom I long devoutly to receive?

3. What can I think on better and more profitable than utterly to humble myself in Your Presence and to exalt Your infinite goodness over me?

I praise You, my God, and I will exalt You forever. I despise myself and cast myself down before You in the depths of my own unworthiness.

Behold, You are the Holy of Holies, and I the greatest of sinners!

Behold, You bow Yourself to me, and I am not worthy so much as to look up to You.

Behold, You come to me, it is Your will to be with me, and You invite me to Your banquet.

You are willing to give me heavenly food and bread of angels to eat,[2] indeed none other than Yourself, that living bread which came down from Heaven and gives life to the world.[3]

4. Behold, from whom this love proceeds! What gracious condescension shines forth here! What great thanks and praises are due to You for these blessings!

How great and profitable was Your counsel when You ordained it! How sweet and pleasant the banquet in which You give Yourself to be our food!

How marvelous is Your work, Lord, how mighty Your power, how unspeakable Your truth!

For You spoke the word and all things were made;[4] and this was done which You Yourself commanded.

5. It is a thing to be greatly wondered at, worthy of all faith, and surpassing human understanding, that You, my Lord God, true God and man, are contained wholly in a little likeness of bread and wine, and so are our inexhaustible food.

You, the Lord of the universe who stand in need of none, are pleased to dwell in us by means of this Sacrament.

Preserve my heart and body undefiled, so that with a cheerful and pure conscience I may be able often to celebrate these mysteries and receive to my perpetual health what you have ordained and instituted for Your own special honor and for an unending memorial.

6. Rejoice, my soul, and give thanks to God for so noble a gift and so precious a comfort left to you in this vale of tears.

For as often as you call to mind this mystery and receive the Body of Christ, so often do you advance the work of your redemption and are made partaker of all the merits of Christ.

For the love of Christ is never diminished, and the greatness of His propitiation is never exhausted.

You should, therefore, dispose yourself to the constant renewal of your mind by attentive consideration of the great mystery of your salvation.

It ought to seem to you as great, as new, and as delightful when you say or hear Mass, as if it were the very day Christ first descended to the womb of the Virgin to be made man; or the day He hung on the Cross to suffer and die for the salvation of mankind.

[1]*Luke 1:43* [2]*Psalm 78:25* [3]*John 6:33, 51* [4]*Psalm 148:5*

Chapter 3

On the Blessing of Frequent Communion

The Voice of the Disciple

Behold, Lord, I come to You so that it may be well with me by Your gift, and I may be delighted in Your holy banquet, which You, O God, have of Your sweetness prepared for the poor.

Behold, all that I can or ought to desire is in You. You are my salvation and my redemption, my hope and my strength, my honor and my glory.

Make the soul of Your servant joyful this day, for to You, O Lord Jesus, I lift up my soul.[1]

I long to receive You now with devotion and reverence. I desire to bring You into my house, so that with Zaccheus I may be blessed by You and be numbered among the children of Abraham.[2]

My soul longs for Your Body; my heart desires to be united with You.

2. Give yourself to me and it is enough, for beside You no consolation avails.

Without You I cannot subsist; without Your visitation I cannot live.

I must, therefore, often draw near to You and receive You for the good of my soul, lest I should faint by the way if I be deprived of this heavenly food.

Once when preaching to the people and healing various diseases, most merciful Jesus, You said, "I will not send them away empty, lest they faint on the way."[3]

Deal in like manner with me, for You have left Yourself in this Sacrament for the consolation of the faithful.

For You are the sweet food of the soul, and he who receives You worthily shall be partaker and heir of everlasting glory.

It is necessary for me, who so often fall and sin and so quickly grow dull and faint, that by frequent prayer and confession and by the reception of Your sacred Body, I renew, cleanse and rekindle myself, lest by abstaining too long, I fall away from my holy resolve.

3. The imaginations of man are prone to evil from his youth,[4] and unless some divine remedy helps him, man quickly falls away to worse things.

Holy Communion draws him back from evil and strengthens him in good.

If I am now so often negligent and cold when I celebrate or receive Communion, what would it be if I did not receive this remedy and did not seek after so great a help?

Although to celebrate every day I am not fit or well prepared, I will endeavor nevertheless at due times to receive the divine mysteries and to be partaker of so great a grace.

For this is the one chief consolation of the faithful soul as long as she is absent from You in this mortal body, that being mindful of her God, she often receive her Beloved with devout mind.

4. O wonderful condescension of Your tender mercy towards us, that You, Lord God, the Creator and Quickener of all spirits, should vouchsafe to come to a poor soul, and with Your whole divinity and humanity should satisfy her hunger.

O happy minds and blessed souls, who have the privilege of receiving You, their Lord God, with devout affection, and in receiving You are filled with spiritual joy!

How great a Lord do they entertain! How beloved a Guest do they bring into their house![5] How delightful a

Companion do they receive! How faithful a Friend do they welcome! How lovely and noble a Spouse do they embrace! even Him who is to be loved above all things that are loved, and beyond all that can be desired.[6]

O most sweet, most Beloved, let Heaven and earth and all that adorns them, be silent in Your presence. What praise and beauty they have is from Your gracious condescension, and can never equal the grace and beauty of Your name,[7] of whose wisdom there is no end.[8]

[1]*Psalm 86:4* [2]*Luke 19:9* [3]*Matthew 15:32* [4]*Genesis 8:21*
[5]*Luke 9:9* [6]*Song of Solomon 2:4* [7]*Philippians 2:9* [8]*Psalm 147:5*

CHAPTER 4

On the Benefits of Devout Communion

The Voice of the Disciple

O Lord, My God, go before Your servant with the blessings of Your sweetness,[1] that I may worthily and devoutly approach Your glorious Sacrament.

Stir up my heart toward You and deliver me from all dullness. Visit me with Your salvation,[2] that I may taste in spirit Your sweetness, which lies abundantly hidden in this Sacrament as in a fountain.

Enlighten my eyes to behold so great a mystery, and strengthen me with undoubting faith to believe it.

It is Your work, not human power, Your sacred institution, not man's invention.

Of himself no man is able to comprehend and understand these things, which surpass the understanding even of angels.

How then shall I, unworthy sinner, dust and ashes, be able to search out and understand so high a mystery?

2. Lord, in the simplicity of my heart, with a good and firm faith, and in obedience to Your commandment, I draw near to You with hope and reverence, and do truly believe that You are here present in this Sacrament, both God and man.

Your will is that I should receive You and that I should unite myself with You in love.

I entreat Your mercy and crave Your special grace to the end that I may wholly melt and overflow with love for You and never hereafter concern myself about consolation, but only You.

For this most high and precious Sacrament is the health of soul and body, the remedy for all spiritual sickness. Here my vices are healed, my passions bridled, temptations overcome or weakened. Greater grace is imparted, virtue already begun is increased, faith is confirmed, hope strengthened, and love kindled and enlarged.

3. You have bestowed and often still bestow many benefits in this Sacrament upon Your beloved who communicate devoutly, O my God, the Protector of my soul, the Strengthener of human frailty, and the Giver of all inward consolation.

You impart to them much comfort to support them in their many troubles, lifting them from the depths of their dejection to hope in Your protection; and You inwardly refresh and enlighten them with new grace, so that they who were full of anxiety and felt no devotion before Communion, after being refreshed with this heavenly food and drink, find themselves changed for the better.

All this You do to Your elect people, so that they may see and know clearly by experience that they have nothing of themselves, but that all the grace and goodness that they have, they receive from You.

For of themselves, they are cold, hard, and undevout; but they are made fervent, cheerful, and full of devotion by You.

Who is there, who approaching humbly to the fountain of sweetness does not carry away from it at least some little sweetness?

Or who, standing by a great fire, does not receive some little heat?

And You are a Fountain always full and overflowing,[3] a Fire ever burning and never failing.[4]

4. Therefore, if I cannot draw out of the full fountain itself, nor drink my fill, I will at least put my lips to the opening of this heavenly conduit, that I may receive from it at least some small drop to quench my thirst, so that I may not wholly wither away.

And if I cannot yet be altogether heavenly or as full of love as the cherubim and seraphim, nevertheless I will endeavor to apply myself earnestly to devotion and prepare my heart to obtain even some small spark of the divine fire, by humbly receiving this life-giving Sacrament.

O good Jesus, Savior most holy, in Your bounty and goodness supply whatever is lacking in me, for You have vouchsafed to call all to You saying, "Come to Me, all who labor and are heavy laden, and I will refresh you."[5]

5. I labor in the sweat of my brow[6] and am vexed with grief of heart. I am heavy laden with sins, I am troubled with temptations, I am entangled and oppressed with many evil passions, and there is no one to help me, none to deliver and save me, but You, O Lord God my Savior, to whom I commit myself and all that is mine, that You may keep watch over me and bring me safe to life eternal.

Receive me to the honor and glory of Your name, You

who prepared Your Body and Blood to be my food and drink.

Grant, O Lord God, my Savior, that through frequenting Your holy mysteries, the fire of devotion in me may grow and increase.

[1]*Psalm 21:3* [2]*Psalm 106:4* [5]*Isaiah 12:3*
[4]*Leviticus 6:13, Hebrews 12:29* [5]*Matthew 11:28* [6]*Genesis 3:19*

Chapter 5

On the Dignity of the Holy Eucharist and the Priestly Office

The Voice of the Beloved

If you had the purity of an angel and the holiness of John the Baptist,[1] you would not be worthy to receive or to handle this Sacrament.

It is not due to any merits of men that a man should consecrate and administer this Sacrament of Christ and receive for food the bread of angels.[2]

Great is this mystery and great is the dignity of priests to whom is given what is not granted to angels.

For only priests duly ordained in the Church have power to consecrate the Body of Christ.

The priest is indeed the minister of God, using the Word of God, by God's command and appointment: but God is the principal Author and invisible Worker, to whose will all things are subject and to whose command everything is obedient.

2. You should, therefore, in this most excellent Sacrament believe God more than your own senses or any visible sign.

Therefore approach this holy task with fear and reverence.

Take heed to yourself, and see whose ministry was delivered to you by the laying on of the bishop's hand.[3]

Lo, you have been made a priest and consecrated to celebrate the Holy Eucharist: take heed that you offer your Sacrifice to God faithfully and devoutly and regularly,[4] and so conduct yourself as to be blameless.[5]

You have not made your burden lighter, but are now bound with a stricter bond of discipline and are bound to a higher degree of sanctity.

A priest should be adorned with all virtues and should give an example of good life to others.

His life should not be like that of common and worldly men,[6] but like that of the angels in Heaven or perfect men on earth.

3. A priest clad in holy vestments assumes the place of Christ, that he may intercede with God for himself and for all the people[7] in a humble and suppliant way.

He has in front of him and behind him the sign of his Lord's Cross, that he may ever be mindful of the passion of Christ.

He bears before him on his chasuble the Cross, that he may diligently behold the steps of Christ and fervently endeavor to follow them.[8]

He is marked with the Cross behind that he may through compassion and the love of God, endure and forgive whatever may be inflicted upon him by others.

He wears the Cross in front, so that he may bewail his own sins, and behind him, so that he may, with true compassion, grieve for the sins of others, knowing that he is appointed to stand between God and the sinner.

He should not be slothful in prayer and the holy oblation till it has been granted him to obtain mercy and grace.

When a priest celebrates, he honors God, he makes angels glad, he builds up the Church, he helps the living, obtains rest for the dead, and makes himself partaker in all good things.

[1]*Matthew 18:10* [2]*Psalm 78:25* [3]*I Timothy 4:14*
[4]*Hebrews 13:15* [5]*I Timothy 3:2* [6]*Philippians 3:20*
[7]*Hebrews 5:3, 7:27* [8]*I Peter 2:21*

Chapter 6

On Spiritual Exercise Before Communion

The Voice of the Disciple

When I consider Your greatness, Lord, and my own vileness, I tremble exceedingly and am confounded in myself.

If I do not come to You, I flee from life, and if I unworthily intrude myself, I incur Your displeasure.

What then shall I do, O my God, my Helper and my Counselor in all necessity?

2. Teach me the right way; give me some brief exercise suitable for Holy Communion.

It is good for me to know how I should reverently and religiously prepare my heart for You, for receiving Your Sacrament to my soul's health or for celebrating so great and divine a sacrifice.

Chapter 7

On the Examination of Our Conscience

The Voice of the Beloved

Above all things, a priest ought to come to celebrate and to receive this Sacrament with very great humility of heart, with prayerful reverence, with full faith and a devout intention of rendering honor to God.

Examine your conscience diligently and to the best of your power purify and cleanse it by true contrition and humble confession, so as not to have or know of anything in you that may breed remorse of conscience and hinder your free access.

Grieve over all your sins in general and in particular bewail and lament your daily transgressions.

If you have time, confess to God in the secret of your heart all the miseries of your passions.

2. Lament and grieve that you are yet so carnal and worldly, so unmortified in your passions, so full of sensual cravings:

So unguarded in your outward senses, so often entangled in vain imaginations:

So drawn to outward things, so negligent of inward and spiritual things:

So prone to laughter and frivolity, so indisposed to tears and sorrow:

So disposed to ease and bodily comforts, so averse to austerity and zeal:

So eager to hear news and to see beautiful sights, so slack to embrace what is humble and low:

So covetous of abundance, so sparing in giving, so tight in keeping:

So thoughtless in speech, so reluctant to keep silence:
So disorderly in manners, so impulsive in action:
So greedy at meals, so deaf to the word of God:
So quick to rest, so slow to labor:
So wakeful to vain conversation, so drowsy at holy vigils:

So hasty to arrive at the end of vigils, so inclined to be wandering and inattentive:

So negligent in saying office, so lukewarm in celebrating, so dry and unmoved at Communion:

So quickly distracted, so seldom wholly gathered within yourself:

So easily moved to anger, so ready to take offense at others:
So ready to judge, so harsh in rebuking:
So joyful in prosperity, so weak in adversity:

So often making good resolutions, and so little carrying into effect.

3. Having confessed and bewailed these and your other defects with sorrow and great displeasure at your own weakness, make a firm resolution always to be amending your life and always to be endeavoring after more progress in holiness.

Then with full resignation and with your whole will, to the honor of My name, offer up yourself a perpetual whole burnt offering on the altar of your heart, faithfully, by committing your body and soul to Me.

Then you may be accounted worthy to come near to celebrate this sacrifice to God, and to receive profitably the Sacrament of My Body.

4. Man has no oblation more worthy, nor any greater means for the washing away of sin than to offer yourself to God simply and wholly together with the oblation of the Body and of Christ in Mass and in Communion.

When a man shall have done what lies in him and is truly

penitent, however often he shall come to me for pardon and grace, as I live (says the Lord, who does not desire the death of a sinner, but rather that he turn and live), I will not remember his sins any more, and they shall all be forgiven him.[1]

[1]*Ezekiel 18:22, 23*

Chapter 8

On Offering Ourselves to God with Christ

The Voice of the Beloved

Of my own will I offered Myself up to God the Father for your sins.[1] My hands were stretched forth on the Cross and my Body stripped and bare, so that nothing remained in Me that was not wholly turned into a sacrifice of divine propitiation.

In like manner, you must also offer yourself willingly to Me day by day in the Mass, as a pure and sacred oblation, with all your strength and affections, and to the utmost of your inward devotion.

What do I require of you more than that you endeavor to resign yourself wholly to Me?

Whatever you give besides yourself I do not regard, for I seek not your gift, but you.[2]

2. As it would not suffice you to have all things without Me, so neither can it please Me, whatever you give, if you do not give yourself.

Offer yourself to Me, and give yourself wholly for God, and your offering will be acceptable.

I offered up Myself wholly to My Father for you, and gave My whole Body and Blood for your food, that I might be wholly yours and that you might remain Mine forever.

But if you stay in yourself and do not offer yourself, your offering is imperfect, and there will not be a complete unity between us.

Therefore, a free offering of yourself into the hands of God must go before all your works if you desire to obtain liberty and grace.

For this reason, so few become inwardly free and enlightened, because they do not wholly deny themselves.

My words stand sure: "Unless a man forsake all, he cannot be My disciple."[3] If you desire to be My disciple, offer up yourself to Me with your whole heart.

[1]*Isaiah 53:7, Hebrews 9:28* [2]*Proverbs 23:26, Philippians 4:17* [3]*Luke 14:33*

Chapter 9

On Offering to God All That Is Ours

The Voice of the Disciple

All things are Yours, O Lord, in Heaven and on earth.[1] I desire to offer up myself to You as a voluntary offering, to remain Yours forever.

Lord, in the simplicity of my heart I offer myself to You this day, to obey You and to become a sacrifice of perpetual praise, to be Your servant forever.[2]

Receive me with this holy offering of Your precious Body, which I make to You this day in the presence of angels invisibly standing by, that it may be for my good and the good of all Your people.

2. I offer to You, Lord, all my sins and offenses which I have committed before You and Your holy angels from the day I first could sin to this hour. I offer them upon Your merciful altar, that You may consume and burn them all with the fire of Your love; that You may wash out every stain of my sins, and cleanse my conscience from every fault,[3] and may restore to me again Your grace which I have lost by sin, forgiving me all my offenses and receiving me mercifully with the kiss of peace.

3. What can I do for my sins,[4] but humbly confess and bewail them and unceasingly entreat Your favor and mercy.

Hear me, I beseech You, in Your mercy.

All my sins are very grievous to me. I will never commit them any more; I grieve and will grieve for them as long as I live, and am resolved to repent for them and to the utmost of my power to make satisfaction.

Forgive me, my God, forgive me my sins for Your holy Name;[5] save my soul which You have redeemed with Your most precious Blood.[6]

I commit myself to Your mercy, I resign myself into Your hands.

Deal with me according to Your goodness, not according to my wickedness and iniquity.

4. I offer up also to You all that is good in me, small and imperfect though it is, that You may improve and sanctify it, and make it pleasing and acceptable to You, and perfect it more and more. Bring me, too, slothful and unprofitable creature that I am, to a good and happy end.

5. I offer up also to You all the holy desires of your faithful servants, the needs of my parents, friends, brothers, sisters, and all those who are dear to me, and all who have done good to me or to others out of love for You.

Also all who have desired me to pray for them and theirs.

Grant that whether they are still in the flesh or are departed out of the world, that all may receive the help of Your grace, the aid of Your consolation, protection from dangers, deliverance from their pain; that they being freed from all evils may return abundant thanksgiving to You with joy.

6. I offer up to You my prayers and intercessions for those especially who have in any way wronged, grieved or slandered me, or who have done me any damage or hurt.

I pray for all those likewise whom I have at any time vexed, troubled, grieved, and scandalized by word or deed, knowingly or unknowingly, that it may please You to forgive us all our sins and offenses, one against another.

Take away from our hearts, Lord, all jealousy, indignation, wrath, and contention, and whatever may wound charity and lessen brotherly love.

Have mercy, Lord, have mercy on those who crave Your mercy.[7] Give grace to them who stand in need of it, and grant that we may be worthy to enjoy Your grace and attain to eternal life. Amen.

[1]*I Chronicles 29:11* [2]*I Chronicles 29:17* [3]*Heb. 9:14, I John 1:7* [4]*Psalm 32:5*
[5]*Psalm 25:11* [6]*I Peter 1:19* [7]*Psalm 123:3*

Chapter 10

That Holy Communion Is Not Lightly to Be Forgone

The Voice of the Beloved

You ought to come often to the fountain of grace and mercy, to the fountain of all goodness and purity, that you may be healed of your vices and passions and be made stronger and more vigilant against the temptations and the wiles of the devil.

The enemy, knowing what great fruit and remedy come through Holy Communion, tries by all means and on every occasion to hinder and draw away the faithful and devout from it.

2. Thus it is that some persons, when they are preparing themselves for Holy Communion, suffer from the harassments of Satan worse than at other times.

The wicked spirit himself, as it is written in Job,[1] comes among the sons of God to trouble them with his accustomed malice, or to make them over fearful and perplexed, so that he may diminish their affections, or by direct assault, take away their faith, to the end that he may cause them either to forbear taking Communion altogether, or at least to come with lukewarmness.

But there is no need to be taken in by these crafty and fanciful suggestions of his, no matter how filthy and hideous they are. Instead, turn all such vain imaginations back on his own head.

You must despise him and laugh him to scorn, and never omit Holy Communion on account of his assaults or of the troubles he stirs up within you.

3. Often too great a care for obtaining a certain height of devotion, and a kind of anxiety about the confession of sins hinder many.

Follow the counsel of the wise in this and lay aside all anxiety and scrupulousness, for it hinders the grace of God and destroys the devotion of the mind.

Do not stay away from Holy Communion on account of every small vexation and trouble, but rather promptly confess your sins and willingly forgive others for whatever offenses they have done against you.

And if you have offended any, humbly ask pardon, and God will readily forgive you.[2]

4. What does it avail to delay your confession and coming to Holy Communion for a long time?

Cleanse yourself thoroughly, spit out the poison with all speed, make haste to take this remedy, and you will find it better for you than if you were to wait a long time to do it.

If you stay away today of one cause, perhaps tomorrow a greater will occur to you, and so you may be kept a long time from Communion and grow more and more unfit.

As quickly as you can, shake off this heaviness and apathy, for it is no use to continue long in uneasiness or with a disturbed conscience, separating yourself from the divine mysteries because of such everyday obstacles.[3]

Yes, it is very hurtful to defer Communion for long, for this usually brings on great lukewarmness.

Alas for sorrow! Some lukewarm and frivolous persons do delay confessing their sins and put off coming to Holy Communion, lest they should be required to keep a stricter watch over themselves![4]

5. How poor and little is their love, how weak is their devotion, who so easily put off Holy Communion!

Happy is he and acceptable to God who so orders his life and keeps his conscience in such purity that he is prepared and well disposed to receive Communion every day if it is in his power, and if it might be done without notice.

If a person should sometimes abstain out of humility, or because of some lawful impediment, he is to be commended for his reverence.

But if a spiritual sloth has crept over him, he must bestir himself and do what lies in him, and then the Lord will assist his intention because of his good intention, for which He always has a special regard.

6. But when any lawful hindrance does happen, he will still have a good will and a reverent intention to receive Communion, and so he will not lose the fruit of the Sacrament.

For every devout person may every day and every hour draw near to Christ without any hindrance[5] in spiritual communion with great profit to his soul.

Yet on certain days and at times appointed, he ought to receive sacramentally with affectionate reverence the Body of his Redeemer, and rather to aim at the honor and glory of God in it than his own consolation.

For he communicates mystically and is invisibly fed as often as he devoutly remembers the mystery of the incarnation and passion of Christ, and is enkindled with His love.[6]

7. He who does not prepare himself except when a feast day approaches or when custom compels him to do so, will often be unprepared.

Blessed is he who offers himself up as a whole burnt

offering to the Lord as often as he celebrates or receives Holy Communion.

Do not be too long nor too brief in celebrating the Eucharist, but keep the accustomed manner of those with whom you live.

You should not inconvenience or weary others, but conform yourself to the received custom, according to the appointment of authorities. Seek the edification of others rather than your own devotion or inclination.

[1]*Job 1:7*
[2]*Matthew 5:23, 6:12-14*
[3]*Luke 15:18*
[4]*Philippians 3:18-19*
[5]*John 15:10*
[6]*II Timothy 2:8*

CHAPTER 11

On the Two Necessities for a Faithful Soul

The Voice of the Disciple

O sweetest Lord Jesus, how great is the happiness of a devout soul who feasts on You in Your banquet, where there is no other food than Yourself, the only Beloved and desirable above all the desires of the heart!

Truly it would be a sweet thing to me to shed tears from the very bottom of my heart in Your presence, and with grateful Magdalene to wash Your feet with them.[1]

But where is that devotion? Where is that abundance of holy tears?

Surely in Your presence and in sight of Your holy angels my whole heart ought to glow and weep for joy.

For in this Sacrament I have You truly present, though hidden beneath another form.

2. My eyes could not endure beholding You in Your own divine glory, nor could all the world endure the splendor of Your majesty.

Here, then, You have regard for my weakness, and veil Yourself under this Sacrament.

Herein I truly possess and adore Him whom the angels adore in Heaven; but as yet I, by faith, while they see with unveiled eye.

I must be content with the light of true faith, and walk in it until the day of eternal brightness dawns on me and the shadows of figures pass away.

But when the perfect is come,[2] the use of Sacraments shall cease, because the blessed need no sacramental healing in their heavenly glory.

They rejoice without end in the presence of God, beholding His glory face to face, and being transformed from glory to the glory of the brightness of unfathomable Deity, they taste the Word of God made flesh, as He was in the beginning and as He abides forever.

3. When I think of these wonders, even all spiritual comfort becomes tedious to me, because as long as I do not behold my Lord in His own glory, I count as nothing whatever I see or hear in this world.

You are my witness, O God, that nothing can comfort me, no creature can give me rest, but You only, my God, whom I long to contemplate forever.

But this is not possible as long as I remain in this mortal life.

Therefore I must be very patient and submit myself to You in all my desires.

For even Your saints, Lord, who now rejoice with You in the Kingdom of Heaven, while they lived, waited in faith and in great patience for the coming of Your glory.[3] What they believed, I believe; what they hoped for, I hope for; whither they have gone, I trust I shall arrive by Your grace.

In the meantime, I will walk in faith, strengthened by the examples of Your saints.

I also have holy books for my comfort and as a mirror of my life, and above all these, Your most holy Body for a singular remedy and refuge.

4. For I find that two things are very necessary for me in this life, without which it would be unbearable.

While I remain in the prison of this body, I confess myself to needing two things: food and light.

You have given me then, weak as I am, Your sacred Body for the refreshment of my soul and body,[4] and Your Word You have set as a lamp to my feet.[5]

Without these two I could not live well, for the Word of God is the light of my soul, and Your Sacrament is the bread of life.

These may be called the two tables set on the one side and on the other in the treasure-house of Your holy Church.[6]

One is the table of the sacred altar, having the holy bread, the precious Body of Christ; the other is that of the divine law, containing holy doctrine, teaching the right faith, and steadily leading even within the veil, to the Holy of Holies.

Thanks be to You, Lord Jesus, Light of eternal Light, for the table of holy doctrine which You have afforded us by the ministry of Your servants, the prophets, apostles, and other teachers.

5. Thanks be to You, O Creator and Redeemer of mankind: You have prepared a great supper to manifest Your love to the whole world,[7] setting before us not the typical lamb to be eaten, but Your own most sacred Body and Blood,[8] rejoicing the faithful with Your holy feast and intoxicating them with the cup of salvation;[9] in which are all the delights of Paradise. The holy angels feast with us, but with even sweeter felicity.

6. O how great and honorable is the office of priests, to whom it is given to consecrate (this Sacrament of) the Lord of glory with sacred words, to bless with their lips, to hold with their hands, to receive with their own mouth, and to administer to others.

How clean should those hands be! how pure that mouth! how holy that body! how unspotted that heart, where the Author of purity so often enters!

Nothing but what is holy, no word but what is good and profitable should proceed from the mouth of a priest, who so often receives the Sacrament of Christ.

7. Simple and chaste should be the eyes that so often behold the Body of Christ; pure and lifted up to Heaven should be the hands that so often handle the Creator of Heaven and earth.

To priests especially it is said in the law, "Be holy, for I, the Lord your God, am holy."[10]

8. Almighty God, assist us with Your grace, that we who have undertaken the office of the priesthood may serve You worthily and devoutly in all purity and good conscience.

And if we cannot live in such great innocence of life as we ought, grant us at least to lament duly the sins which we have committed; and in the spirit of humility, and with the resolution of a good will, to serve You more earnestly for the time to come.

[1]*Luke 7:38*
[2]*Corinthians 13:10*
[3]*Heb. 10:35, 36; 11:39, 40*
[4]*John 6:51*
[5]*Psalm 119:105*
[6]*Ps. 23:5, Heb. 9:2-4; 13:10*
[7]*Luke 14:16*
[8]*John 6:53-56*
[9]*Psalm 23:5*
[10]*Lev. 19:2, 20:26*

Chapter 12

On Preparing Ourselves with Great Diligence

The Voice of the Beloved

I am the lover of purity and the giver of all holiness. I seek a pure heart and there I make my resting place.[1]

Make ready for Me a large upper room furnished,[2] and I will keep the Passover at your house with My disciples.

If you would have Me come to you and remain with you, purge the old leaven[3] and make the habitation of your heart clean.

Shut out the whole world[4] and the clamorous noise of sins. Sit like a sparrow alone on the housetop, and think of your transgressions in the bitterness of your soul.

For everyone who loves will prepare the best and fairest place for his beloved, and herein is known the true measure of his love.

2. Know, nevertheless, that no merit of any action of yours is able to make this preparation sufficient, even though you should prepare yourself a whole year and think of nothing else.

It is solely of My grace and mercy that you are permitted to come to My table, as if a beggar were invited to a rich man's dinner and had no other way to repay him for his kindness but to humble himself and give him thanks.

Do what lies in you and do it diligently, not out of custom, or from necessity; but with fear, reverence, and love, receive the Body of your beloved Lord God, who deigns to come to you.

I am the One who invited you and commanded that it be done; I will supply what is lacking in you. Come, and receive Me.

3. When I give you the grace of devotion, give thanks to your God, not because you are worthy, but because I have had mercy on you.

If you lack this grace and rather feel dry within yourself, be steadfast in prayer. Sigh and knock, and do not give up until you have received some crumb or drop of saving grace.

You need Me. I have no need of you.

You do not come to sanctify Me, but I come to sanctify you and make you more like Me.

You come that you may be sanctified by Me and united with Me, that you may receive new grace and be kindled anew to change.

Do not neglect this grace, but prepare your heart with all diligence, and receive your Beloved into your soul.

4. You ought not only to prepare yourself by devotion before Communion, but carefully also to keep yourself in it after you have received the Sacrament.

A careful guard of yourself afterward is no less necessary than devout preparation beforehand.

For a good guard afterwards is the best preparation for obtaining still greater grace.

If a person seeks too much outward consolation, he becomes less inclined to devotion.

Beware of much talk;[5] remain in some quiet place and enjoy your God; for you have Him whom the world cannot take away from you.

I am He to whom you ought to give your whole self, so that you may now live the rest of your time, not in yourself, but in Me without any anxious care.

[1]*Psalm 24:4, Matt. 5:8* [2]*Mk. 14:14,15; Lk. 22:11,12* [3]*I Cor. 5:7*
[4]*Exodus 24:18* [5]*Proverbs 10:19*

Chapter 13

On Union with Christ in the Sacrament

The Voice of the Disciple

Lord, who will grant me that I may find You alone, to open my whole heart to You, and to enjoy You even as my soul desires, so that none may there deceive me, nor any creature move me nor hold me back, but that You alone may speak to me and I to You, as the beloved desires to speak to his Beloved, and as friend holds fellowship with Friend?[1]

This I pray for, this I desire, that I may be wholly united with You and may withdraw my heart from all created things; that by means of this Holy Communion and frequent celebration of it, I may learn to relish heavenly and eternal things more and more.

Ah, Lord God! When shall I be wholly united with You and absorbed in You, and altogether forgetful of myself?

"You in Me, and I in you";[2] grant that we may so abide forever.

2. In truth You are my Beloved, the choicest among thousands,[3] in whom my soul is pleased to dwell all the days of its life.

In truth, You make peace for me, You in whom is sovereign peace and true rest, and out of whom are labor, sorrow, and endless misery.

Verily You are a God who hides Yourself,[4] and Your counsel is not with the wicked, but Your speech is with the humble and simple.[5]

How sweet is Your Spirit, Lord, who, in order to show Your tenderness toward Your children, vouchsafe to feed them with the most delicious Bread which comes down from Heaven.

Surely there is no other nation so great that has gods so near to it,[6] as You our God are present to all Your faithful, to whom You bestow Yourself as food and drink for their daily solace and to raise their hearts to Heaven.

3. For what other nation is there of such renown as the Christian people?

Or what creature under Heaven is so beloved as the devout soul to whom God Himself comes to feed with His glorious flesh?

O grace unspeakable! O marvelous condescension! O immeasurable love bestowed on man alone!

But what return shall I make to the Lord[7] for all this grace, this charity so without equal?

Nothing that I can give Him will please Him more than to offer my whole heart to God and to unite it intimately with Him.

Then all that is in me shall rejoice, when my soul is perfectly united to God.

Then He will say to me, "If you will be with Me, I will be with you."

And I will answer him, "Vouchsafe, Lord, to abide with me, for I will gladly abide with You. This is my whole desire, that my heart be united to You."

[1]*Exodus 33:11, Song of Solomon 8:1, 2* [2]*John 15:4* [3]*Song of Solomon 5:10*
[4]*Isaiah 45:15* [5]*Proverbs 3:34* [6]*Deut. 4:7* [7]*Psalm 116:12*

CHAPTER 14

On Ardent Desire for the Sacrament

The Voice of the Disciple

How great is the abundance of Your goodness, Lord, which You have laid up for those who fear You![1]

When I remember some devout persons who approach Your Sacrament with the greatest devotion and affection, I am confounded and blush within myself that I come with such lukewarmness, even coldness, to Your altar and the table of the Holy Communion.

I grieve that I remain so dry and without heartfelt affection, that I am not wholly inflamed in Your presence, O my God, and that I am not as greatly attracted and affected as many of the devout have been.

For there have been some, who out of an overwhelming desire and the fervent affection of their heart for Communion, could not keep from weeping. They earnestly thirsted for You, O God, the fountain of life,[2] with a desire both of soul and body. They were not able to satisfy their hunger except by receiving Your Body with all delight and spiritual eagerness.

2. O the truly ardent faith of such souls! It stands as a clear witness to Your holy presence!

They truly know their Lord in the breaking of bread[3] whose hearts burn so fervently within them because Jesus walks with them.

Such affection and devotion as this, such love and fervency are too often far from me.

Be merciful to me, O good Jesus, sweet and gracious, and grant to me, Your needy pauper, to feel at least occasionally in Holy Communion a small portion of Your hearty love, so that my faith may grow stronger, my hope in Your goodness may be increased, and that charity, once perfectly kindled within me after tasting this heavenly manna, may never fail.

3. But Your mercy, Lord, is strong enough to grant me this grace that I so much desire, and in the day of Your good pleasure, to visit me in greatest kindness with an ardent spirit.

For although I do not presently burn with such ardor as those who are so singularly devoted to You, yet, by Your grace I long for this same great and burning desire, praying and longing that I may be made partaker with all who so fervently love You, and be numbered in their holy company.

[1]*Psalm 31:19* [2]*Jeremiah 2:13, Psalm 43:2, Revelation 7:17* [3]*Luke 24:32, 35*

Chapter 15

On Obtaining the Grace of Devotion

The Voice of the Beloved

You ought to seek the grace of devotion earnestly, to ask for it without ceasing, to wait for it patiently and confidently, to receive it thankfully, to keep it humbly, to work with it diligently, and to commit the duration and manner of this heavenly visitation to God, until He comes.

You ought especially to humble yourself when you feel inwardly little or no devotion, and yet you should not be too dejected or inordinately grieved.

God often gives in one brief moment what He has denied for a long time. He sometimes gives in the end what He has deferred to grant in the beginning of your prayer.

2. If grace were always instantly given, and always at hand with a wish, weak man could not well bear it.

Therefore the grace of devotion is to be waited for with good hope and humble patience.

Yet, impute it to yourself and to your own sins when this grace is not given you or when it is taken away and you know not why.

It is sometimes but a little thing that hinders and hides grace, if indeed anything can be called small and not rather a weighty matter, which hinders so great a good.

But if you remove this, be it great or small, and perfectly overcome it, you will have what you have asked.

3. For as soon as you give yourself to God with your whole heart, not seeking this or that according to your own pleasure or will, but settle yourself wholly in Him, you will find yourself united to Him and at peace. Nothing can afford so sweet a relish, nothing can be so delightful, as the good pleasure of the divine will.

Whoever, then, with a single heart, directs his intention to God and keeps himself clear of all inordinate love or hatred of any created thing, shall be most fit to receive grace and ready for the gift of devotion.

For the Lord bestows His blessing where He finds the vessel empty.

And the more perfectly a man forsakes things below, and the more he dies to himself by denial of himself, the more speedily grace comes and the more plentifully it enters and the higher it lifts the free heart.

4. Then he shall see and overflow with wonder, and his heart shall swell within him,[1] because the hand of the Lord is with him and he has put himself wholly into His hand forever.

Thus shall the man be blessed who seeks God with his whole heart; he has not received his soul in vain.

This man in receiving the Holy Eucharist, obtains the great grace of divine union, because he looks not to his own devotion and consolation, but above all devotion and consolation, he seeks the honor and glory of God.

[1]*Isaiah 60:5a*

Chapter 16

On Laying Open Our Needs to Christ

The Voice of the Disciple

O most sweet and loving Lord, whom I now desire to receive with all devotion, You know my infirmities and the needs which I endure: how great are the sins and evils which beset me; how often I am weighed down, tempted, troubled, and defiled by them.

I come to You for remedy; I entreat of You consolation and help.

I speak to Him who knows all things, to whom all my inward thoughts are open, and who alone can perfectly strengthen and help me.

You know what good things I most need, and how poor I am in all virtue.

2. Behold, I stand before You poor and naked, begging for Your grace and imploring Your mercy.

Refresh Your hungering suppliant; enkindle my coldness with the fire of Your love; enlighten my blindness with the brightness of Your presence.

Turn all earthly things into bitterness for me, all grievous and contrary things into patience, all base and unworthy things into contempt and oblivion.

Lift my heart up to You in Heaven, and do not allow me to stray over the earth.

Be my sole delight from henceforth forevermore; for You alone are my food and drink, my love and my joy, my sweetness and all my good.

3. Would that You would wholly enkindle me with Your presence, consume and transform me wholly, that I may be one in spirit with You[1] by the grace of inward union and by the melting of burning love!

Do not suffer me to go away from You hungry and athirst, but deal mercifully with me, as You have often wonderfully dealt with Your saints.

What marvel if I were wholly enkindled by You and should die to myself and come to nothing, since You are a fire always glowing and never dying,[2] a love purifying the heart and enlightening the understanding!

[1]*I Corinthians 6:17* [2]*Hebrews 12:29*

Chapter 17

On Ardent Love and Desire to Receive Christ

The Voice of the Disciple

With deep devotion and ardent love, with all the affection and fervor of my heart, I desire to receive You, Lord, as many saints and the devout have desired You in Communion, who were most pleasing to You in holiness and ardor of devotion.

O my God, eternal Love, my whole Good, my everlasting Happiness, I long to receive You with strong desire, with the most befitting awe and reverence that any of the saints ever had or could feel.

2. Although I am unworthy to entertain all those feelings of devotion, yet I offer to You the whole affection of my heart, as if I alone had all these most thankful and ardent longings.

Yes, and all that a dutiful mind can conceive and desire, with deepest reverence and inmost affection I offer and present to You.

I desire to keep nothing back to myself, but freely and most cheerfully to sacrifice myself and all that is mine to You.

O Lord my God, my Creator and my Redeemer, I desire to receive You this day with such affection, reverence, praise, and honor, with such gratitude, worthiness, and love, with such faith, hope, and purity, as Your most holy mother, the glorious Virgin Mary, received and desired You when she humbly and devoutly answered the angel who declared the mystery of the Incarnation: "Behold the handmaid of the Lord; let it be done to me according to Your word."[1]

3. And as Your blessed forerunner, most excellent of saints, John the Baptist, rejoicing in Your presence leaped for joy through the Holy Spirit while he was yet in his mother' s womb,[2] and afterwards, seeing Jesus walking among men, humbled himself very greatly, and with devout love said, "The friend of the bridegroom who stands and hears him, rejoices greatly because of the bridegroom's voice";[3] in the same way, I also wish to be inflamed with great and holy desires, and to offer myself to You with my whole heart.

Therefore, I offer and present to You the joys, the ardent affections, the raptures, the supernatural illuminations and heavenly visions of all devout hearts, with all the virtues and praises ever celebrated by all creatures in Heaven and on earth, for myself and for all such as are commended to my prayers, that You may worthily be praised and glorified by all forever.

4. Receive, O Lord my God, my vows and my desires to give You infinite praise and boundless blessing, which according to Your unspeakable greatness are justly due to You.

These praises I render and long to render to You every day and every moment. With my prayers and love, I invite and entreat all heavenly spirits and all Your faithful to join with me in giving thanks and praises to You.

5. Let all people, nations, and languages praise You, and magnify Your holy and precious Name with highest joy and ardent devotion!

Let all who reverently and devoutly celebrate Your most sublime Sacrament and receive it with full faith be accounted worthy to find grace and mercy at Your hands, and pray with humble supplication for me a sinner!

And when they have attained their desired devotion and

oyful union, and depart from Your holy heavenly Table well comforted and wonderfully refreshed, may they deign to remember me, a pauper.

[1]Luke 1:38 [2]Luke 1:44 [3]John 3:29

Chapter 18

On Subjecting Reason to Faith

The Voice of the Beloved

You must beware of curious and unprofitable searching into this most profound Sacrament if you desire not to be plunged into the depths of doubt.

He who searches its majesty too closely will be overwhelmed by its glory.[1] God is able to do more than man can understand.

A dutiful and humble enquiry after the truth is allowable, provided we are always ready to be taught and seek to walk in the sound doctrine of the Fathers.

Blessed simplicity! that leaves the way of hard questions and goes on in the plain and sure way of God's commandments.[2]

Many have lost their devotion because they sought to search into things too high.

Faith and a sincere life are required of you, not height of understanding, nor deep enquiry into the mysteries of God.

If you do not understand or comprehend things that are beneath you, how will you be able to understand those which are above you?

Submit yourself to God, and humble your reason to faith, and the light of knowledge will be given to you, as much as shall be profitable and necessary for you.

3. Some are grievously tempted about faith and the Sacrament; but this is not to be imputed to themselves, but rather to the enemy.

Do not argue with your thoughts nor answer the doubts that the devil suggests, but believe the words of God and trust His saints and prophets, and the wicked enemy will flee from you.[3]

It is often very profitable to the servant of God to endure such things.

For the devil does not tempt unbelievers and sinners, whom he already securely holds, but he tempts and troubles the faithful and devout in various ways.

4. Go forward, therefore, with sincere and undoubting faith, and with humble reverence approach this Sacrament; and whatever you are not able to understand, commit without care to Almighty God.

God does not deceive you. He is deceived who trusts too much in himself.

God walks with the simple,[4] reveals himself to the humble, gives understanding to the little ones, opens His secret meanings to pure minds, and hides grace from the curious and the proud.[5]

Human reason is weak and may be deceived, but true faith cannot be deceived.

5. All reason and natural research ought to follow faith, not to go before it or weaken it.

For faith and love especially take the lead here, and work in hidden ways, in this most holy, most supremely excellent Sacrament.

God, who is eternal and incomprehensible and of infinite power, does great and unsearchable[6] things in Heaven and on earth,[7] and there is no searching out of His marvellous works.[8]

If the works of God were such that they might be easily comprehended by human reason, they could not rightly be called marvelous or unspeakable.

[1]*Proverbs 25:27*
[2]*Psalm 119:35*
[3]*James 4:7*
[4]*Psalm 119:130*
[5]*Matthew 11:25*
[6]*Job 5:9*
[7]*Psalm 135:6*
[8]*Isaiah 40:28*

Appendix

Rule of St. Augustine

1. To observe the fundamental law of love, first towards God, then towards our neighbor, according to its just extent, and to imitate the example of the Mother Church of Jerusalem, in union of heart, and sharing with others the goods we possess.

2. To learn the lesson of humility, according to the most perfect pattern set forth in the life of Christ, and in that of his nearest and most faithful followers; and especially in this: that the greatest among them should be as the youngest, and he that is chief as he that doth serve.

3. To observe carefully the stated or canonical hours and times of prayer; and to prepare both body and soul for it by due retirement, meditation, and fasting.

4. To take care that the soul and body be both fed at the same time, by a prudent appointment of some spiritual entertainment at meals, as by reading some sacred book, or by a conference on holy matters, or by singing some devout songs or canticles.

5. To take charge of the sick and infirm wherever they be found, and so far as we are capable, to do them all the service in our power for their bodily and spiritual welfare.

6. To be without any affectation or singularity in dress, and in all other externals of life; and to regard above all things the acquisition of internal purity, and the fashioning of our lives in conformity to the will of God.

7. Humbly and affectionately to give and receive fraternal correction and admonition from one another, meekly to confess our faults one to another, gladly to submit ourselves to the reproof or chastisement of our superiors, and resolutely to keep up the true discipleship of the Gospel.

8. To do all we possibly can for the general good and interest of the community; to be diligent in our duties and callings, never to be idle or wander curiously about, and to be content with the distribution of the common funds, though not altogether so favorable to ourselves as might be expected.

9. Not to neglect outward cleanliness and decency, but to look to the due discharge of outward things for the sake of the inward, and to take proper care of the body for the sake of the soul, both in health and in sickness.

10. To be obedient to our Superior for God's sake, faithfully and kindly to observe our duties toward the other members of the Society, to be ready to ask pardon and to forgive offenses in the spirit of Christ our Lord, but not so as to weaken authority.

Other Christian Classics from Paraclete Press

The Taste of New Wine

Keith Miller

In this modern Christian classic, the author shares, with transparent honesty, the spiritual journey of his heart.

The Story of the Other Wiseman

Henry Van Dyke

Suppose there was another wiseman who, unable to join the three, nonetheless spent the rest of his life on the same quest?

God Under My Roof

Esther deWaal

This collection of Celtic songs and blessings from the oral tradition of the Hebrides evokes a vision of wholeness of life.

Holy Living

Jeremy Taylor

Practical advice on Christian living filled with down-to-earth common sense.

Lead Kindly Light

John Henry Cardinal Newman

A collection of writings of one of the great Christian souls of all the centuries.

Religion of the Heart

Hannah More

A modern edition of Hannah More's advice and counsel—still full of life and wisdom today.

Jesus. Faith ascribes mercy to God with an overplus: 'He will abundantly pardon' (*Isa. 55:7*); 'He will subdue our iniquities; and thou wilt cast all their sins into the depths of the sea' (*Mic. 7:19*). This is faith's language: God pardons with overflowing mercy. A stone thrown into the ocean is not barely covered but buried many fathoms deep. God will pardon your greatest sins, says faith, as the sea swallows a little pebble cast into it. A few sins poured out upon the conscience, like a pail of water spilled on the ground, seem like a great flood; but the greatest sin poured into the sea of God's mercy will never be seen again. Thus 'the iniquity of Israel shall be sought for,' Scripture says, 'and there shall be none; and the sins of Judah, and they shall not be found' (*Jer. 50:20*).

Sometimes, however, the person can be fully persuaded of God's mercy, yet still fear that God's holiness will cut off His pardon for such great sins.

II. FAITH SEES GOD'S HOLINESS AND FORGIVENESS

It is God's holiness which makes Him faithful in all His promises. When the doubting man reads the precious promises given to returning sinners, why cannot he take comfort in them? Surely it is because he is still not sure God is faithful enough to perform them.

But the strongest argument which faith has to put this question out of doubt, and cause the sinner to accept the promise as a true word, rests in the holiness of God, the Promise Maker. He gently persuades the person to trust Him by prefixing His promises with the attribute of holiness: 'I will help thee, saith the Lord, and thy redeemer, the Holy One of Israel' (*Isa. 41:14*). The Hebrew word for 'mercies' is often translated 'holy things,' and because God's mercies are founded in His holiness, they are therefore *sure* mercies (see *Isa. 55:3*). How many times did Laban change Jacob's wages after his